B
ε

D1144449

The Everyday Dancer

The Everyday Dancer

DEBORAH BULL

with illustrations by Millicent Hodson

faber and faber

First published in 2011
by Faber and Faber Ltd
Bloomsbury House
74–77 Great Russell Street
London WC1B 3DA

Typeset by Faber and Faber Ltd
Printed in England by CPI Group (UK), Croydon

A CIP record for this book
is available from the British Library

ISBN 978-0-571-23892-7

2 4 6 8 10 9 7 5 3 1

To everyday dancers, everywhere.

Contents

Prelude

The Everyday Dancer is a book about dancing: what it is, how we do it, what it feels like and what happens when it's all over. Through the structure of a dancer's typical day, the narrative reveals both the everyday schedule and the arc of a dancer's career, from the very first ballet class, through training, to company life, up through the ranks performing both in the *corps de ballet* and as a principal and then, not thirty years after it all began, to the final curtain: retirement, and the sense of loss that comes with saying goodbye to your childhood dreams.

The Everyday Dancer is not intended to be my story, although inevitably I've drawn on my own experiences as a starting point; nor is it intended to portray any single company, any one performance or any particular day. Sharp-eyed readers will recognise elements from certain ballets and may even spot familiar faces within the pages, but the descriptions are intended to be indicative only. In general I've used one personal pronoun – he or she – instead of both, although in many cases (not all) the 'everyday dancer' I'm describing, as well as the choreographers and teachers along the way, could be either male or female. Think Everyman, and forgive those places where I've conflated ballets, people and experiences to paint a clearer picture.

A documentary film-maker once described television to me as 'a series of small lies to tell a greater
truth'. If I've played with some details here it's with
a similar intention – to create an honest account of
what it is to be a dancer. Not the sensational head-
lines, nor the glamorous veneer, just the real, everyday and, at the same time, remarkable experience of
dancing for a living.

Deborah Bull

10.30 – 11.45 Class

It's 28 minutes past 10 o'clock. Around the sides of the studio – leaning against the *barres*, draped across them or stretched out beneath – a group of perhaps thirty dancers is gearing up to do class. They're dressed in an odd array of Lycra, leggings, sweatshirts, chiffon skirts, tracksuit pants, woollen socks and thick fleecy slippers. Legs extend from torsos at unfeasible angles, spines curve backwards and forwards in seamless arcs, calves are massaged, ankles manipulated, tight muscles gently eased. Scrubbed clean of last night's make-up, their faces are drawn, with faint dark shadows below the eyes. Some of them are deep within their own world, intensely focused on their pre-class routine, while others seem to have drifted here on autopilot, not quite ready to focus on anything, not yet. There's a gentle hum of conversation about nothing in particular but the volume, like the energy level, is low. It's not yet twelve hours since the curtain came down on the last performance and in nine hours' time it will go up again, on the next. Class, and the dancer's every day, is about to begin.

Class. It's probably as hard for a dancer to explain class as it is for most people to explain breathing. It's what we do, the ignition key that starts each day. Without class, nothing else happens. It is our daily bread, both rigour and ritual to the dancer, as the Lord's Prayer is to the Priest: an unfailing constant, an inspiration, a reminder of the perfection to which we aspire . . . and, from time to time, an irritatingly repetitive formula it is all too easy to practise mindlessly and, therefore, without any real benefit.

Class is also a great democratiser. Ballet is one of the very few professions in which the most celebrated stars and the humblest of aspirants warm up and take correction together, *en masse*, the Darcey Bussells and the Edward Watsons lined up at the *barre* alongside the newest members of the *corps de ballet* and, sometimes, final-year students from the school. Every morning, regardless of the fact that the previous night's performance may have elevated some of us to superstar status, we are all levelled by participation in this same ritual: the daily class.

In the Beginning . . .

It's a calculated guess, but I'd say that over the course of our dancing lives, between the ages of perhaps seven and forty, ballet dancers will do upwards of ten thousand ballet classes. It starts early, this diurnal ritual, because it has to. It takes ten years to train a dancer: ten years that have to take place before the effects of puberty set in, while maximum flexibility can still be achieved and the necessary neural connections – essential to speed and accuracy – refined. If you want to succeed as a ballet dancer, you'll need to begin taking class well before you reach double figures.

My first classes took place in a local ballet school – the Janice Sutton School of Dance in Skegness – which was (and is) fairly typical of the place where most ballet dancers take their first steps. Set two floors above the fish-and-chip shops and amusement arcades of Skegness High Street, it was a large, wooden-floored room, reached via a steep stone staircase. There was a *barre* running around the sides, but I remember only once being asked to stand alongside it, as I sometimes glimpsed the big girls doing, in their ballet classes. Two solid pillars supported the ceiling and created an obstacle course out of any exercise that wasn't designed to be danced on the spot.

It is in exactly this sort of studio that many of us learn, for the first time, the rudiments of dancing: to curve our hands gracefully, to point our toes, to hold back our shoulders, to turn out our knees and to 'smile, dears, smile'. These first 'official' ballet classes are unlikely to include many of the exercises a dancer will come to associate with daily class over the course of a professional career, but the weekly routine of good toes, naughty toes and simple steps danced to pretty tunes is where it all begins, where the passionate obsession with moving our bodies according to the hard-acquired and long-practised techniques of ballet takes root.

Before long, the once-a-week class has become twice-weekly sessions, with after-school thrown in, until your parents are driving you to and from dance classes most days of the week. By the time you reach double figures, if you're to succeed in this highly competitive profession, you'll have to do what talented eleven-year-olds the world over will be doing: join a full-time ballet school. In today's global market, and with cheap air travel making all the world a possible stage, dancers are hugely disadvantaged if they don't start professional training before they reach their teens. (In some of the newer dancing nations, six- and seven-year-olds are already training for several hours each day.) Generally, this means boarding school, where the waking hours can be maximised and both ballet and academic classes squeezed in to a busy, yet balanced, schedule.

So it was that on 9 March 1974, I was one of a small group of ten- and eleven-year-olds undergoing the annual audition for a place at The Royal Ballet School. Looking back now, I'm not sure that I knew then what I was getting into. I had only ever seen one professional ballet performance, by Ballet for All, a small-scale touring group from The Royal Ballet, which introduced ballet to new audiences up and down the country in the 1960s and 1970s. From the *Princess Tina Ballet Annual* (a cherished Christmas present each year) I had vague notions of ballet companies and a few famous dancers (other than Margot Fonteyn and Rudolf Nureyev; *everyone* had heard of them). But, beyond that, it was all a mystery. From my diary, though, it's clear I understood that this was more than a normal day: every other entry that year in the little beige book (and for several beyond) filled no more than the designated inch of space in the 'week-to-two-pages' format. On 9 March, I added a torn-off scrap of paper, which, though yellowing, remains to this day, tucked into its place. In tiny, spidery writing, I described a scene that reads (but didn't feel) like the one in *Billy Elliot*:

Got up early. Big breakfast at Compton House Hotel. [We had overnighted at a small hotel in London.] 8.30 a.m. went to 153–155 Talgarth Road. 9 a.m. went in. 13 directors in front of us. 8 girls went in. After 3 girls chucked out. In second group to go in, one got through. There was a girl from Hong Kong (Helen). The girls' names I remember are: Victoria, Helen, Kathleen (Christine did not get through). Next all six of us went for another exam (dancing). We all passed this. Then we had an orthopaedic exam. Then dinner. Afterwards they interviewed Kath's parents. Kath did not get in. She was heartbroken. Then my ma and pa went in. I passed. Then we rang my sisters and told them the good news. Looked round London. Came home. Arrived home 10.15 p.m.

The letter of confirmation arrived the following week and, along with eleven other girls and six boys, I became a boarder at The Royal Ballet School – at White Lodge in Richmond Park – on 18 September 1974. (*Breakfast at home, set out at 9.20 a.m. Settled in easily. Played tennis after supper. Watched telly. Wrote to Mum.*) From that point onwards, class was a different story. No more good toes, naughty toes. At The Royal Ballet School, we did class 'properly' – which is to say we did it according to a format we would follow until the end of our dancing careers.

The Dancer's Environment

Ballet class is remarkably similar the world over (and because the steps are all described in French, it's usually possible to follow a class in any country, whether you speak the language or not). More than a format, it can justifiably be described as a ritual. The ritual plays out in a studio specially designed, or at least adapted, for the purpose. It will, ideally, be spacious and unencumbered by random pillars and it will have a sprung floor with a certain amount of 'give' built in, to ease the dancers' descent from jumps and protect the ankles, knees and spine. On top of the wooden boards, these days, you're likely to see a covering of grey or black linoleum. A smoother surface, with less potential for turning an ankle at the point where one board meets another and no possibility of splinters, lino is cheaper to replace and (arguably) less slippery than wood. The ubiquitous resin box in the studio's corner – the foot-square tray filled with powdered resin around which dancers would cluster, scratching their feet like chickens in a farmyard – is now, largely, a thing of the past. Resin crushed into the soles of *pointe* shoes effectively dealt with the slipperiness of wooden floors but, strangely, does exactly the opposite with lino.

The walls of the studio will be lined with floor-to-ceiling mirrors and, ideally, curtains that can be pulled across to conceal them; dancers can become addicted to their own reflections. Put in the same room as a mirror, a dancer will find it hard – almost impossible – to resist. Our eyes will be drawn over and over to our own image, never mind that this is likely to distort the movement we're trying to perfect. We imagine that the mirror is helping, but it's like all addictions: the addict is convinced it offers support but, in the longer term, it's undermining your ability to stand (quite literally) on your own two feet – or, more usually, one.

Mirrors are dangerous because, given the choice, the brain will always prioritise the information it receives via the eyes: it's far more interesting than the information it gets from the sensors in our muscles, ligaments and joints, through proprioception. But proprioception – or at least, an enhanced ability to deal with the information proprioception provides – is the dancer's secret weapon. Staying upright – never mind moving – requires a constant stream of minute corrections to your posture: balance is not a static condition. (Try to stand on one leg and feel how the muscles around your ankle joint make rapid adjustments to keep you from falling over.)

Through training, dancers become expert at sensing their position and making these adjustments so quickly that they can't be seen: the better the dancer, the more 'still' they appear. Correcting mistakes based on what you see in the mirror, rather than what you sense via your body's feedback systems, is a slower and less effective process and, besides, there are no mirrors on stage. Of course, this is the science, and I knew none of it for most of my dancing life. If I had, I might have taken more seriously the requests not to look at myself in the mirror during class.

The only other notable feature you'll find in the ballet studio, parked in one corner, is a piano. From the time I started at White Lodge, throughout my training and my entire career, I can count on the fingers of two hands the number of times I did class without live music (and always then on holiday or out of hours) and I remain inexpressibly grateful to the men and women whose musical skills and versatility helped me through those classes when I would much, much rather have stayed in bed.

Outside the larger schools and professional companies, it is all too rare to find a pianist and not a CD accompanying class. Presented always with a recording, with the same melodies and rhythms, the dancer executes movements and sequences at exactly the same tempo, day after day, week after week. Imagine only ever driving the same route between your house and office, always with the same weather conditions, the same oncoming traffic, the same light and the same parking space at each end. You might (rightly) question whether you could actually drive at all.

While the extra salary for a pianist continues to make live music an impossible luxury for most ballet schools, ballet studios have definitely gone upmarket since I started to dance. Even Janice Sutton has moved, to a purpose-built studio away from the pervasive odour of fish and chips, with its own stage, changing rooms and a car-park. For The Royal Ballet, we lived through an almost unimaginable transformation when, in 1999, the redevelopment of the Royal Opera House, part funded by the National Lottery, delivered five full-sized studios for The Royal Ballet, just an elevator's ride away from the stage. Prior to that, we'd divided our time between rehearsals in the three studios at Barons Court, twenty minutes away, along London's Piccadilly line, and stage calls and performances at the Royal Opera House, in Covent Garden. But even we had it easy compared with our predecessors.

In the 1930s, in the company's early days as the Vic-Wells Ballet, its studio had to be vacated well in advance of curtain up as it doubled as the public tearoom at Sadler's Wells Theatre in Islington. When I first joined the company, before the new studios were built, the principals would take class before stage calls at the Royal Opera House in a small, windowless room just off the basement canteen, while we *corps de ballet* dancers clung to a makeshift *barre* along the centre of the Crush Bar (as it was then), struggling to hold our turn-out against the slippery surface of the red carpet. If nothing else, it was very strengthening for the inner-thigh muscles.

Look in on The Royal Ballet in class these days and you will see airy, spacious studios, lit naturally from above, a cool architectural abstraction of white walls and pale lino, its purity sullied by an animated jumble sale of ragbag outfits. The breathtaking physical elegance of the dancer is undermined, in every instance, by our bizarre clothing culture. The messier, the odder, the baggier, the better – or so it would seem. In fact it's far more subtle than that. Ballet clothing and ballet culture have both undergone a massive change over the last three decades and one is, almost certainly, a manifestation of the other.

Photographs of ballet companies in the 1940s and 1950s show the men tidy, in black tights and fitted T-shirts, and the girls clad in pink tights no longer good enough for performance, but darned in the 'make-do' spirit of the post-war years. On top, they wore big knickers and short tunics, tucked in around the knicker line at the front to create what looked like a leotard, with a tiny skirt at the back modestly lapping the line of the buttocks. Waists were marked with a wide belt, necklines demurely rounded, hair pulled neatly back into buns or held in place by scarves. Knees were, without exception, wrinkly: it would be another thirty years, at least, before Lycra changed all that. Between rehearsals and classes, handknitted crossovers and leg warmers might be added, but leaving them on once work had begun was seen as pretty bad form. (This is, in fact, exactly the uniform we wore in our first year at The Royal Ballet's junior school, although the pink tights were replaced with Brettles shell-pink ankle socks and if our knees were wrinkly, well, that was our own fault.) While there was never an official uniform for the ballet company, the look was, most certainly, uniform: a combination of post-war rationing, limited availability, team spirit and Englishness. And, of course, a physical manifestation of an art form where uniformity is, in some ways, a goal. No uniformity, no *corps de ballet*.

In my days in the company, uniform was, most definitely, *not* the look we were aiming for. In fact, we managed to achieve it, with fashions such as long T-shirts, fleece babygrows, machine-knitted woollen shorts and the like spreading as fast in the studio as trends catch on in the playground. But, below the surface, it was all about individuality: necklines hacked for maximum flattery; leggings cropped to just the right length to emphasise good points and disguise the bad; printed slogans, scarves and wispy chiffon skirts. We were (just) the children of the Thatcher years, brought up to see individualism as our birthright and determined to proclaim it – even while we were all dancing the same steps.

In truth, these seemingly random outfits were often

carefully selected security blankets. Christine Wood-ward, a senior *corps de ballet* member when I joined the company – memorable for her faultless profes-sionalism and razor-sharp wit – once quipped that this must be how dancers spent their rare days off: stationed in front of a mirror, scissors poised, choos-ing and then marking exactly the angle at which a cropped T-shirt had maximum effect, or where leg warmers crossed the line from emphasising a shapely ankle to highlighting a bulky calf. I always suspected there was some truth in this, that the absent-minded chic of a dancer's wardrobe was the result of anything but chance.

Some of us were better than others at achieving the right look and I never seemed to arrive at an indi-vidual style, the way Alessandra Ferri did, with her spider's-web-thin woollen shawls draped casually around her gamine hips, or Jonathan Cope, with his vaguely Masonic one-legged tracksuit pants. (I did spend quite a lot of time trying a variety of guises to pass off my English pear shape as something more Continental. It was only when I finally gave up the struggle that I realised no one else minded it quite as much as I did.)

So forget Degas and his pastel picture-book perfec-tion. This is the snapshot you will see, if you peep into the window as class at the Royal Opera House is about to start: no rococo gilt, no wooden floors, and no tulle skirts, but a late twentieth-century architect's sparse vision of a calm, austere landscape marred – or perhaps improved? – by brightly coloured bodies, positioned at regular intervals around the edges of a vast, airy space. Each one is poised, left hand on the *barre*, attention half focused on the teacher who seems to be making hand signals to accompany a short volley of *franglais*. 'OK girls: two *demi*, one *grande*, *port de bras*, rise, balance and change position. First, second, fourth and fifth. Two bars in. And . . .' Let class begin.

The Teacher

The teacher taking the class is usually, but not always, an ex-dancer and, for the next seventy-five minutes, her position in the studio is all-powerful. The teacher sets the tone of the class. She is responsible for engendering a healthy working atmosphere, an environment of respect, not fear. She must set exercises that are challenging but not overwhelming; clearly communicate the musical requirements to the pianist; give corrections; notice where dancers are in difficulty and adjust accordingly; and pace the class so that the dancers are fully warm but not exhausted by the end. A good teacher should have wisdom, patience, kindliness, charisma – and energy and enthusiasm in the face of a room full of exhausted dancers, barely recovered from the show the night before. It's not surprising that not all teachers entirely live up to this ideal.

While dancers are training, it's usual to have the

same ballet teacher for a sustained period of time. Back at The Royal Ballet School, we had a specific teacher for each of the seven years, with two – Patricia Linton and Nancy Kilgour – staying with us for two years each. They were some of the most inspirational and passionate teachers I would ever know. Throughout the years of training – at least up to the age of sixteen – a dancer is still acquiring the basic technical tools and so there is a need for continuity and structure across the weeks, months and years. Professional dancers (while always having room to improve) have already mastered the 'curriculum', if such a thing exists, of classical ballet technique and so, in a company, while consistency over a specific period can be useful (for instance, hiring a Balanchine specialist to teach class while the company learns and stages *Ballet Imperial*) it is not absolutely essential.

Rotating the teachers between classes over the course of a week can help to keep the dancers stimulated and engaged, particularly during a long run of performances. In The Royal Ballet, we had two or three 'resident' teachers at any one time during my twenty years: Brian Shaw, a fine ex-dancer who taught textbook classes, very correct, very 'square' and very English; Gerd Larsen, a beautiful Norwegian who had already taught the company for ever when I joined and whose performances in the great character roles – Giselle's Mother, for instance – were masterclasses in the oft-neglected art of mime; Alexander

Agadzhanov, who brought with him from his native country all the positive and classy hallmarks of Russian training at its best; or Betty Anderton, an ex-dancer with The Royal Ballet and Festival Ballet, full of energy and a better tonic in the morning than anything you'll find behind the counter in Boots. Guest teachers would come and go, finding favour with the dancers or not, depending as much on the levels of exhaustion in the company at the time as on their skills in the studio.

At the Barre

Whoever the teacher, class begins, invariably, at the *barre*. Expressed in French, like all ballet terms, this one is self-explanatory. (Unlike some: *gargouillade* – literally, a gurgle or rumble – is a favourite.) *Barre* means bar. And it is just that, a rounded wooden pole attached to the walls of the studio by metal brackets, just below average shoulder height and just large enough to prevent an entire hand closing around it like a fist. The *barre* should be lightly held, not grabbed: it is there as a reminder, not as a lifesaver. (We were always taught that the thumb should rest towards the top surface of the *barre*, close to the four fingers, rather than grasping the underside as if your hand was clasped around a can of beer.)

Almost without exception, class starts with the left hand on the *barre*, leaving the right leg (the working leg) towards the centre of the studio and free to exercise. I have never found out why this should be the case, but it remains an unwritten rule, along with turning towards the *barre* between exercises, rather than changing sides by turning towards the centre. Go figure.

Over the next seventy-five minutes, the dancers will be 'put through their paces' in a series of exercises that are almost identical in form to the ones that ballet dancers the world over have practised since ballet technique was codified, in 1820, by Carlo Blasis, probably the most important ballet teacher of the nineteenth century. Based initially on instinct and refined through evolution rather than hard science, these exercises have, nevertheless, proved remarkably efficient in training the human body in the specific practice of ballet.

The aim of these exercises is twofold – another oddity particular to ballet. For ballet class sets out to do two things at once: it is the mechanism by which dancers warm up and, at the same time, the way in which they improve their basic technique. Little by little, the exercises increase in speed and intensity, elevating the heart rate so that it pumps more blood (and therefore more oxygen) to the working muscles and raising the body temperature so that muscles become warmer and therefore more pliable. At the same time, the dancer is striving to improve technique, to increase turn-out, to find a cleaner *arabesque*, a faster *pirouette* or a lighter jump. In contrast, most singers would warm up for performance with a calculated selection of scales, arpeggios and the like, not by singing a selection of phrases plucked from well-known arias. But ballet class (the dancers' warm-up) is – in part – just that: the steps may be grouped differently and set to different tunes, but they are the very same steps that make up ballets such as *Sleeping Beauty* or *Giselle*.

Ballet technique is based on a series of positions of the arms and the feet that was first formalised by Pierre Beauchamps, dancing master to Louis XIV, in 1661. To most people, these five basic positions are relatively familiar – or, at least, familiar enough to be parodied on mainstream television (French and Saunders had a particularly good try).

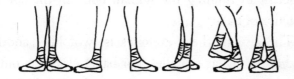

First position of the feet has the two heels touching, with the legs rotated and the toes pointing outwards, in a Chaplin-esque 'ten to two' (or, these days, quarter to three). In second, the feet retain exactly the same relationship to each other, except that the heels are separated – so the feet shift sideways, leaving roughly the length of one and a half feet as a gap between the two heels. Simple. Third, where the heel of one foot slides close in front of the other, comes next –

except that it's pretty much obsolete these days, used only in teaching young children before they are strong enough to graduate to the more complex fifth: ballet's equivalent of the stabilisers on a kid's bike. Fourth can be either 'open' (from first position, slide one foot forward, keeping the heels in line with each other) or 'crossed' (the same, but the front heel crosses the body so that it is opposite the toes of the back foot).

Fifth, the tightly crossed position that appears to narrow two legs to one beneath the dancer's centre – heel of the front foot snuggled alongside the toe of the back foot – is the subject of much debate. Should the toe of the back foot be peeping out from behind the front or should the foot in front completely conceal the other? Should the knees be absolutely taut (physically impossible for some anatomies) or is a little relaxation allowed? Sensible teachers advocate approximating the ideal within daily class and rehearsals only as far as one's individual anatomy allows. From time to time, in performance, you might need to force yourself into the perfect fifth position, if the choreography absolutely demands it. But that would be for fractions of a second, and on a few occasions a year. That much, you can probably get away with: the potential for damage inherent in twisting and forcing yourself hundreds of times a day, 365 days a year, doesn't need explaining.

I'm forever grateful that I was trained by teachers who, perhaps unconsciously, but nevertheless consistently, put the laws of anatomy before the laws of the stage. Their mantra was that you work within the capacity of your own body, striving little by little to :end that capacity, but always remaining within the ounds of your own physical limitations. Muscles and ndons can be stretched; bones cannot. Other schools of thought advocate that for each position there is an absolute – a state of perfection that each dancer *must* achieve, never mind the physical cost – but it's a method of teaching that favours the physically blessed. Fortunately, by the time I encountered this way of thinking, I was a little too old to try and a little too wily to believe that I ought.

Aside from the positions of the feet, and a corresponding set for the arms, a series of basic principles applies across ballet technique and throughout class:

· The legs are always rotated outwards in the hip sockets, creating the 'turn-out' particular to ballet
· The feet are pointed whenever they are lifted from the floor
· The weight of the body is carried slightly forward, over the balls of the feet rather than on the heels
· The muscles of the legs, stomach and buttocks are active, pulling the body upwards, away from the floor, like a cat ready to pounce
· The hips remain level and 'square' to the front, the two hip bones in line, like the headlights on a car
· The ribcage is flat, not puffed up like a budgerigar's
· The shoulders are relaxed – but held in place so that they cannot roll forwards

- The arms are carried slightly forwards of the body so that whichever position they take, except those directly behind the body, they can be seen within the dancer's peripheral vision
- The arms are never rigid: in every position exce arabesque, they are slightly rounded with the elb lifted
- The fingers are grouped together, with the thumb tucked gently in towards the palm and the second finger (the longest) drawn slightly down, towards the thumb
- The neck is relaxed and the head and eye line raised very slightly above the horizontal

And all this before *barre* can begin.

What's in a Class?

The seventy-five minutes or so of class are divided between exercises at the *barre*, exercises in the centre (sometimes called 'centre practice') and *allegro* (jumps, both small and large). The proportion of time allocated to each segment varies from teacher to teacher – and depends to some extent on the level of the students – but, on average, *barre* is accomplished in around thirty minutes, with another twenty dedicated to centre practice and the remainder of the class spent jumping.

The type of exercises, and the order in which they are done, is more or less standard. Class always starts with *pliés* – except when it doesn't. It did, for the first fifteen years of my dancing life, but a quiet and partial revolution in class format coincided with *glasnost* and the early 1980s. Suddenly, there was no need to defect in order to leave Russia and so, for the first time since before the Revolution, a group of influential teachers from the Bolshoi and Maryinsky traditions became a regular feature on the international dance scene. They brought with them some positive innovations to the format of class, including the pre-*plié* warm up exercise, facing the *barre*, the equivalent of a gentle massage for the feet and knees before the more taxing business of class proper begins. Perhaps these feline preparations for the lower limbs (think of a cat kneading and pawing its owner's lap) came about originally because Russian studios were often so cold but they have lived on here, in the centrally-heated West. Freed from a slavish commitment to *pliés* as the morning's first move, some dancers and teachers now precede class with Pilates, massage, or a work-out on an exercise machine – all of which may be a safer and more appropriate start to the day than a full *plié*, a deep 'squat' with knees at full flex that puts tremendous pressure on joints that are not fully warm.

After *pliés*, *barre* generally unfolds in a standard sequence: *battements tendus, battements dégagés, ronds de jambes à terre, battements fondus, battements frappés, ronds de jambes en l'air, petits battements, adagio, grands battements* and then a few moments and thirty-two bars of music in which to stretch. Even now, a full seven years after my last professional class, the list rolls off my tongue via my fingers and on to the page without engaging my conscious brain. Yet while the sequence may be standard, the possible variants on each individual exercise are seemingly limitless.

Imagine yourself standing by the *barre*, left hand attached, and facing along its length. You are free to move your right leg forward, to the side, or to the back. You can also move your left leg (the one nearest the *barre*) to the front and back and, at ground level only, to the side. (Any higher and you'd kick the wall.) You can bend forwards and backwards and to both sides, over the *barre* and away from it. Even a *battements tendus* exercise, a simple sliding of the foot from the closed position to a stretched, pointed extension and then back again, can be done in an almost infinite range of permutations and so, before each exercise, the teacher must either explain or demonstrate to the class the combination she has planned.

The exercises start gently, feet close to the ground and at a relatively sedate pace. Over the course of the *barre*, they increase in speed and in range, until *grands battements* sees legs thrown high in the air – in my day, beyond shoulder level; these days, above the head. Each exercise is, in some way, preparing the body for the demands that are to follow, in the centre of the room and, later, on stage and, in particular, for jumping. *Ronds de jambes à terre* and *en l'air* increase the rotation of the leg in the hip joint, extending turn-out. The melting action of *battements fondus* mimics in slow motion the pushing off and landing from a jump, as do the much faster and more strident *battements frappés*. *Petits battements*, with the working foot wrapped around the ankle of the standing leg, is a preparation for the crisply beating legs of *entrechats*.

Each exercise is set by the teacher and learned quickly, from a set of instructions offered only once. ('Two to the front, and pick, pick, close, repeat with the inside leg to the back, same to the side, brush back, and front and back and close. Reverse, and then we'll turn quickly around and go immediately on the other side. Slight breath between the legs, please' – the last, unintended, double entendre a request to the pianist to hold up slightly while we turn to begin again on the other side.)

Between the exercises, there may well be a pause while an individual is given a correction or a more general point made to the class as a whole. Depending on the complexity of the teacher's exercises and the generosity of the corrections, the thirty minutes of *barre* time can incorporate up to ten minutes' talking. Left to their own devices, dancers could cover a pretty comprehensive *barre* and be fully warmed up in about a quarter of an hour.

Once *barre* is over, the class moves to the centre of the room where the dancers form loosely structured 'lines', usually facing the mirror. Back at White Lodge, the lines were anything but loosely structured: arranged in alphabetical order, with four to each row, after each exercise the girls at the front would peel off and move to the back, affording each row its place in the sun and the teacher better scrutiny of the dancers' efforts. Companies, in my experience, are nothing like so formal. Dancers each have a comfort zone: some prefer to be close to the front, others favour the safety and security of the back corners, but each will find a convenient square foot of space – usually the same as the day before, and the day before that – and settle in for the centre.

The first exercises of centre practice mimic those at the *barre* to some extent: *ports de bras*, *battements tendus*, *adagio* and *grands battements*. If the class is large, the teacher may divide the dancers into two groups and the non-active group will slope off to the sides, practising, stretching or (less recommended) chatting. Some of the women may choose to change into *pointe* shoes at this stage: either to break in a new pair, or because there is little point in mastering the remaining exercises of the class on half-*pointe* when, on stage, you will almost always be required to dance them on *pointe*.

It's about 11.15 now. With half an hour still to go, there is a noticeable shift in the pace and structure of the class. The mass of bodies gathered in the centre disperses and regroups in the right-hand back cor- ner. A waltz begins and, as the first *pirouette* exercise starts, the steps of the classroom become more closely associated with the choreography of the stage.

Pirouettes

Dancers either love *pirouettes* or they hate them. I've done both. When I was at school, back in the 1970s, a good, clean double turn was all our teachers ever expected of us. Later on, in the company, we had fun, after class, trying to outspin the boys, but bringing anything beyond a double to the stage wasn't considered particularly good form. (I once did four *pirouettes*, by accident, in Balanchine's *Serenade* and was reprimanded by the ballet mistress who left me in no doubt that this kind of ostentatious display was, well, a bit *cheap*.) But at some point during the late 1980s and early 1990s, these implicit spin restrictions were relaxed, as dancers trained in different methods and with different mindsets arrived at The Royal Ballet. We locals could only stand by in amazement as a succession of dancers (notably the Spanish) rotated on one leg for longer than we had ever imagined possible. The ability to turn wasn't, after all, a genetic inheritance: it was clearly a technique that could be taught.

Even so, it's not the easiest movement to analyse and, try as you might, it's not easy to figure out where the momentum for the *pirouette* actually comes from. A *pirouette* might look like a spinning top, but it's not powered by the same impetus: you spin a top by twisting it first in the opposite direction. In a *pirou-ette*, there is no swing to the left before a turn to the right. So the only force available comes from the *plié* beforehand: when you push up from bent knees on to *pointe*, the energy of the upward thrust is converted into a rotation, creating the turn. Gathering the arms into a closed position, like a skater, adds to the effect and enhances the spin. (At least this might be how it works: it's the best theory we came up with when I spent time analysing *pirouettes* with a physiologist.)

The dancer avoids dizziness by 'spotting': focusing the eyes on a single spot, directly to the front, and leaving the head as long as possible during each turn before whipping it round sharply to arrive back at the same point. This whipping action prevents the fluid in the inner ear from building up momentum (as it would, otherwise, when you turn around repeatedly) and effectively tricks the brain into thinking you're not spinning at all, hence minimising the dizzi-ness. So spotting during turns is essential and in a dark theatre, where visibility is low, you spot anyway, even if you're forced to imagine a point in the middle distance. (The obligatory illuminated exit signs can come in handy, if there's one where you need it.)

Allegro

After a couple of *pirouette* exercises, class takes another new direction, with the first jump. Generally, this part of class starts with a quick warm-up exercise, with all the dancers back in their square foot of space. Typically, in this first exercise, the jumps will take off from, and land on, two feet and may be nothing more than a series of springs in a single position (first and then second) concluding with a series of *changements*, springs in which the dancer alternates between one fifth position (right foot in front) and the other (left foot in front). Once feet, ankles, calves and knees are prepared, the more complicated *enchaînements* begin: sequences of jumps that travel or turn, taking off from, or landing on, one foot rather than two. These types of jumps are much harder and more tiring and, potentially, more dangerous, particularly when you build in beats or changes of direction.

Young dancers will add these embellishments little by little, and only when the teacher believes the class is ready. Seasoned professionals, unless they are injured, take all these things in their stride, although an observer may note that the class starts to shrink in size round about this time, as dancers who have an early rehearsal, a persistent physical niggle, shoes to sew – or who are just plain exhausted – make their excuses and slip away. For those who stay, the pace and the level of exertion build: this is the part of class that most resembles the choreography of the classics, particularly for the men. *Enchaînements* get longer and more complex, incorporating the show-stopper tricks of the repertoire: *tours en l'air*, double *sauts de basques*, *grands jetés*, and *jetés en tournants* around the room.

Human muscle tissue divides into two types. We all have both – and dancers are no exception – but in differing proportions (with the hare and the tortoise the most extreme and best-known examples). The difference is particularly evident here, in the *allegro* section of class. Those dancers with a predominance of fast twitch muscle fibres appear light and springy, landing from each jump and rebounding sharply, like a power ball. They burn bright, but tire quickly. The dancers with more slow twitch muscle fibres are strong and have better endurance, but they can appear a little more laboured when they jump. The ratio of slow to fast twitch fibres is hard to influence, as are the other factors that contribute to a good jump: length of tendons, and the relative proportions of foot and lower leg that make for effective 'levers'. So while dancers *can* improve their jump (largely by increasing their muscle strength and thereby improving the power-to-weight ratio), changes are relatively slight and very hard to achieve. If you're good at jumping, don't be too pleased with yourself. You can probably thank your parents.

With big jumps over and the clock edging towards 11.45, the class stops as unceremoniously as it started, with a 'thank you' from the teacher and a genuine but distracted smattering of applause from the dancers. Mostly, we have moved on in our heads and are already considering the rehearsal which is to follow, the costume fitting, the role we have to learn or the phone calls we need to make. And while it might have looked like performance, it was nothing of the sort. However impressive they might have seemed to a non-dancer pausing by the studio's window, the double *tours* and the leaps and the multiple *pirouettes* were nothing more than the everyday prelude to the dancer's day.

12.00 – 1.30 *Corps de ballet* Rehearsal

Ten minutes after class ends, the dancers of the *corps de ballet* are back in the studio, flat shoes exchanged for *pointe*, damp leotards for dry and, perhaps, a practice tutu or chiffon skirt added on top to mimic the costume of the ballet they're about to rehearse. The early arrivals set up camp beneath the *barres*, dumping handbags, water bottles, leg warmers and tote bags full of *pointe* shoes at the sides and to the back. The front is left clear: the *répétiteur* and the notator are already installed there on two upright chairs, discussing the shape the rehearsal will take.

The energy levels in the room are higher now than they were before class began, ratcheted up in direct relation to the temperature of the dancers' bodies. A group of six or seven are up on their feet, going over the complicated counts, the *port de bras* or the traffic flow at the point where the choreography weaves one line of dancers through another. (Left crosses in front of right: it's another of those conventions.)

Rehearsals may take place in the same studio, with the same dancers hard at work and the piano still in its corner, but they are not the same thing as class. Class is a formulaic process, recognisable the world over, designed both to warm the body and to polish up basic technique. Rehearsals are where existing ballets are practised and new ones created, where the alphabet of the ballet language, perfected through class, is put to work building the phrases, sentences and chapters of ballet's many stories. Now, class over, the mirror to the studio's front represents the theatre's auditorium and the *barres* at the side and to the rear mark the backcloth and the wings, from which entrances are made and where exits conclude. The studio is re-imagined as a replica of the stage.

As the minutes tick by, the last few stragglers trail in, finishing phone calls, bananas and cans of sugary drinks. Plasters are hastily added to tender toes, shoes changed. At 12 noon, the *répétiteur* draws everyone's attention to a focal point centre front with a clap of the hands: 'OK, let's go from the beginning of the second movement . . .'

First Rehearsals

Most dancers' first ever rehearsal is a world away from this everyday picture of life in a busy ballet company. It probably takes place at their local dance school, as preparations get under way for a summer special, or a Christmas show. My first rehearsals were in the same studio in which I learned my very first steps: the Janice Sutton School of Dance in Skegness. In the summer of 1971, we were rehearsing for a run of performances of *The Wizard of Oz*, at the nearby Derbyshire Miners' Holiday Camp, and I was practising to be a Smartie in the Kingdom of Sweets. Forty years on, I can recall the garden slide down which we slid, like sweets poured out of the tube, all dressed in Smartie-coloured leotards with short, perfectly round PVC skirts and matching hats.

I remember that Mum asked Janice if I could re-use a purple leotard I'd worn the year previously, to save the expense of buying another. But Janice was a stickler for verisimilitude and in those days purple Smarties were still to be invented. Mum got around the additional expense by making a pink leotard for me, out of brushed nylon (well, it was the 1970s). The fabric had all the elasticity of a brick wall (and a tendency to create sparks, too) and I can still recall its stubborn refusal to 'give' as I arched back or extended a leg behind me. It was the first of many occasions on which I'd have cause to feel guilty about the expense to which a career on the stage puts a dancer's parents.

But while I can picture a too tight leotard and a garden slide, I don't remember what I *thought* of those early rehearsals, or how I felt. (As my diary writing didn't start until 1974, the year I went to White Lodge and put the Derbyshire Miners' performances behind me, I have no way of finding out.) I know that I always loved (and still do) the sense of communal achievement that comes from rehearsing and the creation, over weeks and sometimes months, of temporary, large-scale families with a common goal at their heart. Perhaps the bigger girls envied Debbie Jenner, Janice's star pupil, and the fact that she always got the lead role, but we younger ones were just happy to be involved. There was no sense of rivalry among us at all: as far as I knew, I was the only little girl from Skegness who had decided that she was going to be a ballet dancer. I imagined the others were simply there to have fun.

Rehearsals: Ballet School

At White Lodge the atmosphere was different: we had all decided we were going to be ballet dancers. Nevertheless, the sense of shared purpose and of us all being 'in it together' remains with me more vividly than the competitiveness that surfaced, inevitably, from time to time. Every year, the school presented summer performances, at the nearby Richmond or Wimbledon Theatres, as well as an annual Matinee at Covent Garden. This (much grander) performance was really for the Upper School students but included (and still does) White Lodgers in a display of folk and national dances. The real prize, however, was to be selected to be a rat (good) or one of the children (much better) in The Royal Ballet's Christmas performances of *The Nutcracker*.

I never featured in the folk and national dances at Covent Garden. Neither did I make it as one of the *Nutcracker* children, failing an audition that took place just two weeks after we arrived at White Lodge for our first year. 'Too tall', the official verdict; 'not quite good and/or cute enough', the likely truth. (*1 October 1974: 'Auditions for* Nutcracker. *Wrong size. Two letters!'*) The disappointment was clearly short-lived and two letters from home warranted as much coverage in the diary.

It was around that time, aged eleven, that we began to learn the harsh truth of a dancer's life: that sometimes you'll be chosen and sometimes you won't, and that it won't always be possible to see, or understand, why. And we began to experience a more slippery truth, too: that to you, some people will appear to be chosen all the time and to others, *you* will appear to be the one with all the luck. In neither case is this actually true. American psychologists probably have a name for this syndrome.

In the spring of the following year, Elisabeth Schooling – a student of Marie Rambert and, from 1930, a member of her company – came to White Lodge to mount a ballet called *Jeux d'Enfants*. Set to music by Georges Bizet, it was, literally, a series of children's games, made up of short dances with titles such as 'The Seagull', 'The Doll', 'The Hoop' and 'The Streamer'. My diary for 1975 records the moment I discovered I was involved.

Friday, 28 February: School. In eve we changed to mufti and played in garden. I was called for rehearsal!! I was by the pool, and Miss Schooling said – aren't you meant to be in rehearsal? So, I said *No!* and she asked my name and said she had put my name on the board and said – get changed!!

The performances of *Jeux d'Enfants* were to take place at the end of the summer term, on 18 and 19 July, and I was cast as part of the *corps de ballet* – in which section, I don't remember. This probably represents the longest rehearsal period I had throughout my entire career: almost five months – although Easter holidays would have taken a chunk out of that and rehearsals were limited to at most an hour a day, fitted around the regular dance activities and 'normal' school curriculum. A month before the performances, I was called on, at short notice, to fill the gap left when a fellow student was injured. The exclamation marks in my diary entry are a poor representation of the dizzy excitement I still recall.

16 June 1975: *Jeux* rehearsal. Miss Wadsworth said I had to learn Streamer!! (cos Louise and Karen are both off.) So, I'm covering Streamer.

Fast-paced, vivacious, and with sequence after sequence of bounding jumps, the Streamer was one of the central roles and Karen Gee was the perfect dancer for it. (I knew Karen from the annual Dance Festivals, in Skegness and nearby Cleethorpes. She was the strongest dancer in our class at the time and would later become a Principal with English National Ballet.) I still remember the music and much of the choreography, even now, thirty-six years later. It started with a swooping run on from the wings and then, centre stage, two *sissones* forward, two back, two *temps de cuisse* from side to side and a *soutenu* . . . The next day, Miss Wadsworth, the second year's teacher, went through the solo with me, but it turned out I already knew it – absorbed, seemingly, by osmosis.

I began to rehearse it every day in the studio and endlessly in my head, at night. I'd stay awake long after lights out, going through the steps in intricate detail. In my imagination, each one was executed perfectly, every musical nuance enhanced, every technical challenge surmounted. And then, each day in the studio, I'd fail to bring this nocturnal vision to life. It was agony. I knew I could do it. I remember wishing I could summon Miss Schooling in the night, go down to the studio and show her there and then just what I could achieve. The sense of frustration I felt then at this inability to make public my better self remains with me, vividly, even now.

It wasn't to be. In the end, Louise and Karen recovered to share the performances and I rejoined my friends in the *corps de ballet*. In my diary, I'm remarkably sanguine about the way things turned out. Sometimes you're chosen, sometimes you're not. Sometimes, you're chosen – briefly – and then, once again, you're not. *Jeux d'Enfants* was an early introduction to the ups and downs of a dancer's life.

Rehearsals: The Graduate Student

For a student at The Royal Ballet School, the first experience of proper, professional, *corps de ballet* rehearsals takes place during the final year at the Upper School, aged seventeen or eighteen. The Upper School, back then, was based alongside the company at 153–155 Talgarth Road, the place where we had all auditioned in what by now seemed like an earlier life. Although we shared the building, there was a clear division between company and school: the professionals had their own studios and changing rooms, their own dining room (although the canteen itself was shared), their own 'nerve centre' (a suite of tightly packed offices with notice boards outside) and, most notably, they had no uniform. While we students dressed in regulation black (year 1 and 2) and burgundy (graduate class), there were no such restrictions on the company.

It was around this time that Lycra made its debut on the world stage (about a decade too late for my Smartie episode) and with its unique ability to cling tightly to contours, to stretch (hallelujah!) and to be dyed in a rainbow of colours, it changed the dancer's wardrobe for ever. This was before the days of grunge (and with Nicholas Dixon and Ashley Page the exception, punk had failed to impact on The Royal Ballet's dancers) so the soloists – Pippa Wilde, Deirdre Eyden, Genesia Rosato – all tended to capitalise on, rather than conceal, their already stunning beauty. Unbearably glamorous, with their breathtakingly perfect forms shimmering in baby blue, peach or bright white all-overs, we could only gaze in open-mouthed awe as they passed us in the corridors.

The two worlds might have been clearly defined, but we found ourselves constantly crossing between them, as we students entered the graduate year and began to take part, as last-resort covers, in the company's *corps de ballet* rehearsals. By the time it was our turn, we were well aware of the process and how it worked, having watched friends in the class above go through it all a year earlier. Perhaps this explains the element of expectation about it that my diary reveals and the absence of any of the sense of delight I would imagine now that I felt then, at finding *my* name on a Royal Ballet cast list.

Thursday, 25 September 1980: we finished at 5.15 p.m., when a company extra list went up on the board. I'm doing *Giselle* Wilis and *Swan Lake* Peasants – I'm very pleased. I'm not doing Swans.

In *Giselle*, I would later discover, I covered Jacqui Tallis (perhaps the first dancer whose name I ever knew, thanks to a feature on her in one of my *Princess Tina Ballet Annuals*). The next day, a second list went up, for Fokine's *The Firebird*: '*I'm actually in it, as a bride, and I cover the Wives. I'm very pleased,*' I write – 'very pleased' being the only suggestion of praise I'll apparently allow myself to record.

We learned all these roles not with the company, but in 'Repertoire' (Wednesdays, 1.30–2.30, with Lynn Wallis), part of the graduate-class weekly schedule. The aim of these 'rep' classes was twofold: to introduce us to the specific skills required to dance as a group, and to arm us with a working knowledge of The Royal Ballet's repertoire in advance, so that by the time we went into rehearsals with the company – if we were lucky enough to be selected – we would already be familiar with the steps and polished to some degree of perfection by Miss Wallis, whose impossibly sleek, black hair (achieved before the days of straighteners) and immaculate daily make-up served as advance warning of her passion for perfection. She drove us hard and had no time for slackers, instilling in us the collective discipline on which a successful *corps de ballet* depends.

Largely, the repertoire classes did their job, although sometimes the timing was slightly out and company rehearsals began before we had fully absorbed the choreography. And you couldn't, of course, assume that the place you'd learned, in a routine that might feature twenty-eight dancers, was the one that the company would ask you to cover. And so you tried to keep your eyes everywhere in rep classes, picking up the general shape and patterns of the choreography, and everyone else's steps as well as your own.

According to the diary, my first ever rehearsal with the company was on Tuesday, 30 September 1980, as a Wife, in *The Firebird*. I don't recall – nor does my diary comment on – how I felt as, together with my 'chosen' classmates, we slipped into the back of the studio and tried, simultaneously, to be invisible *and* to ensure that the company staff noticed how well we were doing. I'm surprised, looking back, to see from the following pages how quickly we found ourselves in among the company dancers. The very next day, 1 October, I stood in for Gail Taphouse in Peasants (*And I only knew half of it. Still, everyone was really helpful*') and Julie Lincoln in *Firebird* (*Again, everyone was very kind*').

As it turned out, it didn't seem to make a difference whether we were official covers or not. Sometimes you're chosen; sometimes you're not. Sometimes you're not chosen but you still find yourself up there and doing it:

Tuesday, 4 November 1980: After the rehearsal, Miss Gregory [Jill Gregory, Ballet Mistress for The Royal Ballet] told me that tomorrow, at the Dress Rehearsal, I have to do Bryony's place in Act II swans, as Glen Tetley wants her at Barons Court. [Tetley was creating a new piece, *Dances of Albion*, and had chosen a very young Bryony Brind as second cast to Lesley Collier.]

Wednesday, 5 November 1980: Dress Rehearsal! Arrived early at the Royal Opera House to do my make-up – we had to go in the Ballet Room. After class with Gerd Larsen, we started. I had to do Peasants, which was fine, then Act II swans, which was OK too. As I started to remove my make-up and hair, Sharon McGorian said to me: 'Oh, I wouldn't do that if I were you. You may have to do Act IV.' I explained that I didn't know Act IV – and that I don't even cover Swans. So she offered to teach me some of the steps during Act III and I bravely did Act IV – It was fine. I didn't make any mistakes and I *literally* just followed Sharon and Vicky. They told me to run, wave my arms, or *bourrée* to the left, or follow Sharon during 'Boot Hill', etc., and I just did it. And I've never learned any of Act IV before in my life. Jill Gregory said I was very good!

Throughout the graduate year, participating in rehearsals and performances became a regular feature in our schedule, allowing the ballet mistress and the company management, as the months went by, to form an opinion on whether or not each of us might be a fit with the company. Like most of my classmates, I didn't ever think about whether or not the company would suit me: I'd decided that aged eleven. Later on, as I struggled to make my mark in the company, my diary does, on occasion, question whether I'd be better to try my luck elsewhere, but the question was always asked half-heartedly, as if I knew that I was exactly where I wanted to be.

Company Rehearsals: Fully Paid and Fully Paid Up . . .

With so much exposure to the company and its working practices during our time as students, life as a professional felt very familiar. It seemed to revolve around the notice board (or boards) outside the company offices, where sheets of A4 paper, closely typed and carbon-copied, ruled our every move. Inclusion in, or omission from, the cast lists and rehearsal calls provoked disappointment and delight, in equal measure.

I remember three boards in the Barons Court corridor, taller than me, wider than a row of swans and covered in deep red felt. Working from right to left, the first was the repository for a random selection of information from a variety of sources, and the only place we dancers (as opposed to management) were allowed to pin up notes.

The central of the three boards had the week's timetable, a single page per day, pinned side by side across the board's width. The calls were posted on Friday, at noon, for the following week, and we would cluster around, noting the times we were required into our diaries and notebooks. The call sheets started the week in black type on white paper and then, as dancers were injured and casting changed, ended up a mass of red-ink annotations, as if a child had been let loose with the felt-tip box.

The board on the left held all the cast sheets: each page of A4 had the ballet's title at the top, centred, and then character or role names in a column down the left-hand side, starting with the principals, followed by the soloists and ending up with the *corps de ballet*. Each role was followed by a space and then (and here was the important bit) the surnames of the dancers cast to perform.

In those days, the casting was in order. If your name came first, you were 'first cast' and you could assume you would be dancing the opening night. After the names of those who were cast came, in brackets, the names of the covers. The brackets were a kind of metaphor: the dancers positioned in the brackets would be the ones standing in the wings during the show, watching, learning, absorbing, hoping . . . Covers, then as now, would not expect a performance, but were wise to be ready to go on at a moment's notice, as often happens. *Next day on your dressing room they've hung a star . . .* We never give up hoping.

At the foot of the page, stationed between more of the symbolic brackets, was a list of names making up a general pool of understudies for the *corps de ballet*. This was the least prestigious part of the page to be and, in my first week of professional life, this is exactly where I found myself: general cover for the *corps de ballet* in Balanchine's *Serenade* and, consequently, jostling for space at the back of a studio packed tight with other dancers dancing.

Scheduling the Calls

In a busy ballet company, there can be up to 120 rehearsals in an average week. The scheduling of all these rehearsals, of varying length, scale and style, is a complex, multi-factored feat that should have been made easier with the development of computer software but that still relies on a high level of personal familiarity with the repertoire, the individual dancers and the *répétiteurs* involved.

Before you can begin to schedule rehearsals for any particular ballet you need to know how many acts or movements it has, how those sections are made up and how demanding they are, how long each lasts as well as how many people are in the cast. You have to be able to make a judgement about whether it can be rehearsed on the same day as other ballets with differing physical demands. (Ballet dancers are extremely versatile, but it doesn't make physical sense – it can even be dangerous – to go straight from a rehearsal of a strictly classical piece into something using contemporary technique, such as *Rite of Spring*.)

You need to remember that on Wednesday, for example, the *corps de ballet* has a particularly heavy evening show and that asking them to rehearse Swans and Nymphs all day will probably tip them over the edge. You need to know whether dancer A will be happy with a 5 o'clock slot, and whether dancer B rehearses with *répétiteur* C. You need to remember that dancer D doesn't much like studio A, and that studio B is slightly too small for the end section of ballet E. Oh, and dancer F is doing guest performances in Buenos Aires and so won't be available until the following week.

And then, with all those considerations and a few dozen more held in the front of your brain, you have to shoehorn the many sections of the ballet into the available studios (five at the Royal Opera House), rehearsing up to six different casts over the course of perhaps three or four weeks – at the same time as the company is performing two different programmes and rehearsing three more. Unsurprisingly, the role of scheduler has never been advertised at the local job centre and has always, to date, been undertaken by a former dancer with the sort of brain that finds cracking the Rubik's cube (a) interesting and (b) a possibility. So much for the notion that dancers' brains rest entirely in the tips of their toes.

In the Studio: Répétiteurs

The *répétiteur* (literally, the 'person who rehearses', or the coach) is almost certainly a former dancer, too. He or she will probably have been that dancer who always knew everyone else's steps, the one who had the patience to explain the choreography to a newcomer just one more time, the one who took the initiative to arrange quick backstage rehearsals when someone went off at the last moment. Over time, the management will have noticed these qualities and started to entrust this dancer with more and more responsibility, perhaps even giving him an official 'assistant' title and a salary increase. Finally, when a vacancy arose for a *répétiteur*, he will have been offered the job (in my day) or applied, been interviewed and then employed (in these more transparent times).

A company such as The Royal Ballet, with around ninety dancers, will have several *répétiteurs*, some with responsibility for the *corps de ballet*, some who rehearse the soloists and some who coach the principals. On top of this, guest *répétiteurs* will be engaged for specific ballets – by George Balanchine, or Jerome Robbins, for instance – or when an unfamiliar work from another company is imported into the repertoire.

The role of *répétiteur* is a coveted one, for many reasons. A dancer who cares about traditions, standards and quality will find himself, as *répétiteur*, in a unique position to pass on the wisdom of generations, to maintain the high standards for which a company is famous and to help younger dancers to develop their individual skills. And a *répétiteur*'s career is longer than that of a performer. With most dancers forced to consider retiring at a very young thirty-five to forty, the job of *répétiteur*, feasible for a further twenty years, starts to look particularly attractive.

But it's a role that comes with a whole raft of responsibilities. First, you have the hopes and aspirations of each of those young dancers in your hands, on a daily basis. And then consider those standards and traditions: each time a ballet company performs one of the cornerstones of its repertoire it is compared with, and judged against, every other performance in living memory (and then a few more that no living person actually saw but which are the stuff of legend). In my time, the spectre of the *Evening Standard* award-winning *Bayadère* corps of 1974 hung over us every time we trembled our way down the ramp to enter the Kingdom of the Shades. Spirits haunted by super spirits. A good *répétiteur* has to inspire respect for those standards and traditions while understanding that each generation brings its own values to the process and has its own contribution to make to the evolution of dance.

In the Studio: Learning and Remembering

Rehearsals can last between thirty minutes and three hours, depending on the ballet in question and on where you are in the journey between first rehearsals and opening night. Typically, the first rehearsals of a ballet – the 'learning' rehearsals – will be scheduled to last slightly longer than the later calls, perhaps two or even three hours.

Of the dozen or so programmes in a ballet company's year, up to 90 per cent might be revivals and so ballets are generally being remembered rather than learned from scratch. From time to time, a company will take a work into the repertoire that has been successful elsewhere (John Cranko's *Onegin*, for instance, acquired by The Royal Ballet in 2001). And there are the ballets brought out of mothballs: *Coppélia*, a staple of the repertoire in the company's early years that didn't feature at all in my two decades with The Royal Ballet, revived in 2001, or Frederick Ashton's *Sylvia*, rescued from near-extinction in 2004 after an absence of almost half a century. More usually, a ballet is 'rested' for a few years only and so when it returns to the repertoire there is always *someone* in the company who has danced it before and has memories of the choreography on which to draw.

To an outsider, the first rehearsals of a ballet would probably appear to be rather slow and inconsequential, fractured movement phrases interrupted by some head scratching and sections repeated over and over again as we struggle to claw back the physical sensation of choreography that has not been danced – or even thought about – for months, if not years. It's hard – even for the dancers involved – to see the connection between these early studio calls and the polished performance of the first night.

Some dancers are better than others at recalling once-familiar steps from dusty memory stores. Frequently we remember, but not quite accurately, swearing we did a step on the left leg when the evidence (a video, for instance) proves it was on the right. When ballets are long out of the repertoire, dancers are likely to remember the rhythm and dynamics of the choreography rather than the exact steps, certain that it went 'di dum, dum dum, and three and four', but unsure exactly what *it* was. Interrogating the memory too consciously can cause it to retreat for ever into some distant corner of the brain, and too many questions usually prove fatal. ('No, no, don't ask, just let me do it for you.') Even now, as I try to recall snippets of choreography from my dancing years, I know that I'm best placed to do it as I'm falling asleep at night, when my conscious brain is a bit less 'on duty' than it is during the day.

We talk a lot about getting things 'into our bodies' and it's true that when we really know a ballet, it seems to be stored directly in our muscles and not in our brains. But while 'muscle memory' is a good way of describing how it feels to dance a well-rehearsed role, it's not accurate. The body doesn't function like a memory-foam mattress, storing shapes and movements as indentations within its lean tissue. What 'muscle memory' probably means is that the steps have been repeated so often, and over such a long period of time, that the skill has become unconscious, their 'memory' moved from the front of the brain to the cerebellum. When you dance these highly familiar steps, it feels as if your body is doing them on its own, without any reference to the conscious brain, as if you're dancing on autopilot. This is a vital stage in progressing from fumbling first rehearsal to expert performance, and it leaves the frontal cortex free for the important business of interpretation and interaction with the other artists on the stage.

In the Studio: The Notator

With so much potential for misremembering (and, in the case of *corps de ballet* roles, up to thirty-two possible versions to choose between) it's invaluable to have someone on hand to rule on the definitive version. In the larger ballet companies, this is probably the notator, or choreologist: the person trained to write down, to read and to interpret the choreography in a dance notation score.

The notator is integral to company life but nevertheless cuts an anomalous, slightly distant figure in the studio. With his constant referencing of books and a professional reliance on an academic skill, the notator is somewhat at odds with ballet's long tradition of steps passed verbally from master to pupil, down several generations of a big dancing family. Despite this culture – or perhaps because of it – the search for an accurate and reliable method of writing down choreography goes back to the very beginnings of ballet.

As early as the 1670s, Louis XIV ordered his dancing master, Pierre Beauchamps, to develop 'a way of making dance understood on paper'. Surviving attempts to come up with a universal system date as far back as 1844, when Arthur Saint-Léon developed 'La Sténochorégraphie'. The great dancer and choreographer Vaslav Nijinsky experimented with notation, as did many others along the way, but the format war was finally declared a draw in the mid-twentieth century, with the winners being Labanotation (created by Rudolf Laban in 1928) and Benesh Notation, published in 1956. The other methods – the Betamax,

Squariels and HD-DVDs of the notation world – were consigned to history, fondly recalled by just a few specialists in the field.

Benesh Notation has long been The Royal Ballet's principal method of recording choreography. It was devised by Rudolf Benesh (by profession, an engineer) for his wife Joan, a dancer in the company, who complained frequently at home about the number of steps she had to remember at work. Benesh's logical system was created in 1955 and adopted by the company in 1960. Written on staves of music – and therefore directly related to the relevant musical score – it uses a series of dots, dashes, crosses and curves to build a complete representation of movement that can record every element of a dance: where the dancers are on the stage and in relation to others, where they are facing or travelling, what each part of the body is doing and in what rhythm and at what speed.

At The Royal Ballet School, we learned notation from the age of thirteen onwards. The master plan was that, over time, dancers would become as comfortable with dance notation as musicians are with scores, that we could be given our homework to study overnight and we would return the next day, step perfect. Imagine the efficiency! It didn't quite work out like that, but notation – in the hands of expert notators – has, nevertheless, an invaluable place in the recording and remembering of choreographic texts.

It would be easy to imagine that digital technology and the ubiquitous video camera will render notation obsolete, but this is unlikely to be the case. Despite our best efforts, dancers can't be relied on to repeat the choreography with textbook accuracy every time we perform, so you can't depend on a single filmed performance being the ultimate record of a choreographer's intentions. This could be for any number of reasons: injury, exhaustion, a 'bad day' (we do have them), or straightforward memory lapse. The notation, written down in the studio as the choreographer is creating the ballet, can provide a complete and accurate record of the steps.

What strokes on a page struggle to capture is the impetus or drive behind a movement: its accuracy is, of necessity, rather clinical. I've always believed that the best record of all is a combination of three elements: a living link to the original work (the *répétiteur*, a dancer who performed the role or the choreographer himself), a filmed record of performance and, of course, a notator armed with the score.

Rehearsing the Corps

Once the choreography has been taught, or remembered, the rehearsals are handed over to the ballet mistress (or master) who is responsible for bringing the *corps de ballet* up to standard, ready for the full calls and, eventually, for the stage.

The range of styles and techniques the *corps de bal-let* has to master across the repertoire is vast, from the strictly classical, danced in geometric patterns and with military precision, through highly stylised character dances, to contemporary choreography where none of the usual rules apply. Some *corps* numbers involve both the men and the women – the peasant dance in the first act of *Swan Lake*, for instance – but the major-ity of the *corps de ballet* dances in the classical ballets are for the women alone: Swans, *Sleeping Beauty*'s Nymphs, *La Bayadère*'s 'Shades', the *Nutcracker* Snow-flakes and more. It is in these sections that the *corps de ballet* plays its unique role – a mass of human bodies moving as one – and it is in this type of choreogra-phy that the requirement for discipline, inherent in a dancer's training, is most clearly understood.

Corps de ballets operate in even numbers. Depend-ing on the ballet, there are usually between twelve and thirty-two dancers involved in its *corps*. Classical bal-let, like all the classical art forms, is based on sym-metry, with the *corps de ballet* on one side of the stage frequently mirroring the *corps* on the other, or fanning out in both directions from the centre, like the wings of the Palace of Versailles. The choreography might move in and out of geometric formations, a direct link to the origins of classical ballet and the 1581 *Ballet Comique de la Reine*: in this first ever *ballet de cour*, the dancers formed circles, squares and triangles to demonstrate how reason and geometry bring order to the universe and help to raise man closer to God and spiritual harmony. At other times, the *corps* might provide a frame for the principals at the centre of the stage, forming groups around them or working in lines parallel to the wings.

Jean-Georges Noverre, ballet master and author of the highly influential *Lettres sur la danse et sur les ballets*, published in 1760, proposed that ballets should function like paintings rather than plays: these human *tableaux* have their roots way back, in Noverre's theories. Sometimes, the choreography for the *corps* is highly symbolic, the entrance of the *Bayadère* Shades snaking back and forth across the stage like the lazy smoke from an opium pipe, or the *corps* in *Swan Lake* forming a phalanx and advancing on the audience with arms waving up and down in unison: a vast and majestic swan in flight.

Despite the individual ambition to dance alone – an ambition most dancers harbour, at least at the beginning of our careers – the challenge and the skill here is to dance as one: to stay directly in line, backwards and forwards as well as side to side; to mirror the shape, line and angles of the dancer ahead; to replicate exactly her timing and musicality; to lift legs, arms, or eye line only to the height the dancer at the front of the line dictates. In a perfect *corps de ballet*, no one dancer stands out.

And in a good *corps*, all of this is second nature. You learn quickly to have eyes everywhere; you learn to restrict your exceptional jump or your outstanding *arabesque* – if you have one. Sometimes newer members may need to be prompted to check the line sideways as well as forwards, or to swivel their eyeballs discreetly to the side to ensure their arm is at the same height as their neighbour's. Sometimes even the more seasoned *corps de ballet* dancers have to be reminded to run on the balls of their feet, or to turn out the leg nearest the audience as they do so, to prevent their downstage foot appearing the length of a ski.

But leaving these reminders aside, rehearsals are not generally about perfecting the skills of the *corps*. The bulk of the time is spent perfecting the work in question: its technical challenges and its particular style. Some ballets – *Giselle*, for instance – are romantic in style: arms are soft like wings, heads gently inclined, the mood submissive. In classical ballets such as *Sleeping Beauty*, the posture is upright, the carriage poised and self-assured, the chest open and arms held proudly, adorning each position like a crown. The *corps*, through its dances, is responsible for setting the style of the ballet, preparing the ground for the principal dancers who follow.

Over the course of rehearsals, once the dancers have the choreography 'in' their bodies, the ballet mistress will run each section from start to finish, over and over, to build the stamina required. Although dancers retain a high base level of fitness during the season, some *corps* numbers have specific demands – they might be particularly long, or be made up entirely of jumps – and it's through these daily rehearsals that the dancers build the strength they will need, not only to perform to the best of their ability, but to recover within seconds their breath and composure.

For the *corps*, there is no possibility of gasping for air, hands on hips, bent double in the wings. When their number is over, the dancers of the *corps* are likely to remain on the side of the stage, standing on one leg in a formal line or grouping, poised and unmoving for the next five or ten minutes, while the soloists and principals take their time in the spotlight.

Full Calls

At the same time as the dancers of the *corps de ballet* are perfecting their particular sections, the soloists and principals are scheduled into the other studios to rehearse their parts. A fortnight or so before the first night, we all meet up, in the largest of the rehearsal studios, for the first of the 'full calls': a three-hour run-through of the entire ballet in which all those separately rehearsed elements will be pieced together. With up to eighty or ninety dancers in the room, plus stage managers, pianist and conductor, it has the atmosphere of a town square on market day. Along the front of the studio there are now perhaps four or five members of the ballet staff: *répétiteurs* for the *corps*, soloists and principals, the ballet mistress, the notator and possibly the company director, too.

Stage management has set up the studio in advance to resemble, as closely as possible, what we'll experience on the stage. Tape markings on the floor indicate where the edges of the set will be and easily transportable props have been brought up to the studio. Odd bits and pieces are called on to stand in for the more unwieldy items, an orange plastic chair doubling as a throne, a music stand and a stool marking the palace gates. With this mock-up set in place and the edges of the studio resembling the shoreline following high tide – an unimaginable flotsam and jetsam of bags, garments, bodies, bottles and shoes strewn all around – the rehearsal begins.

Voices are raised louder than before – they have to be – and the atmosphere is workmanlike, pragmatic, with moments of sheer magic taken a little for granted. Each element has been well rehearsed by the time we come to put them together in a full call, but the joins between them may need a little polishing and the principals can, at times, get tangled up in the *corps de ballet*. In most cases, their set pieces are relatively stand-alone, but in both *Sleeping Beauty* and *Swan Lake* there are *pas de deux* danced among Nymphs or Swans and it's inevitable, in these first full calls, that paths will cross.

As far as is possible, the ballet will be run in sequence with one cast and then, over the course of the following days, most of the casts will have a chance to rehearse the entire work with the full company. Principals might choose to cut their solos if they're tired, or nursing an injury, or if time is running short, but where solos are danced full out, they're likely to earn applause from the *corps*. In my early years in the company, this was frowned on, particularly by Michael Somes – distinguished male dancer and partner to Margot Fonteyn and, later, Principal *Répétiteur* – who thought it over-indulgent.

Step by step, section by section, we limp through from beginning to end. Three hours is a long time and even with a fifteen-minute break, blood-sugar levels can drop, tempers can fray, dancers can fall and difficult steps can be fluffed. It's a bit rough on day one, but by the second full call, it begins to feel like a show.

Stage Calls

The final rehearsals of a ballet take place on the stage, over the course of the two or three days leading up to the first night. With stage calls starting at around 10.30 in the morning, class can be shifted to the unsavoury hour of 9.30 – a particular hardship when we might not have finished until 10.30 the night before. (I remain, even now, allergic to early starts, the 10.30–10.30 working day set too firmly on my internal clock.) As opening night comes closer, the class gets even earlier: for the dress rehearsal, we might have to be ready in make-up and wigs in advance of a 9.15 class.

The first stage call can be a bit of an anti-climax. The stage might be relatively bare, with only 'indicated' sets available. Without lighting, it all looks a bit sad, the colours slightly muted, the fakery a little obvious and its impact dulled. On day one, the rehearsal staff is likely to sit along the front of the stage, lined up like the VIPs at a prize-giving ceremony, but facing the wrong way. With all this, and the piano still standing in for the orchestra, the move to the stage can feel a little premature, as if we might as well still be upstairs in the studios, without the early start.

As the days go by, different elements are added into the mix until, on the final day, it all comes together in something that looks very much like a performance: sets, props, costumes, make-up, wigs, lighting, orchestra, the lot. For the dress rehearsal, there might even be an audience, of sorts, made up of students from The Royal Ballet School, or the Friends of Covent Garden. The ballet runs without stopping, as it will on the night. Applause follows each section. The curtain goes up and down, intervals are observed, and we rehearse the line-up for the calls, if not the calls themselves. Almost a performance, but not quite. Tonight, it happens for real.

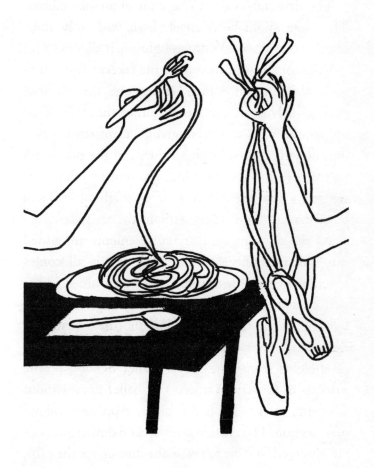

1.30 Lunch

Lunch, for a dancer, is a movable feast. Well, perhaps not quite a feast, but it's certainly movable, in more senses than one. First, it's unlikely you'll ever find the time to eat a conventional lunch, sitting at a table, knife and fork in hand. More often than not, you'll pick out something portable and eat it on the move. Second, the lunch break itself is likely to dance around in the schedule. Some days, you'll have an hour's break early, at midday; others, it will be a very respectable 1.30. If you're very unlucky, you might work straight through from noon until 3 o'clock before you can stop for something to eat.

With so much work to cover – for The Royal Ballet, around 135 performances of fourteen different programmes each season in London and an additional twenty-five on tour – leaving the studios empty for an hour in the middle of the day while we all down tools is not an option. Across five studios, that would make for five wasted hours. And so the schedule dictates that we head to the canteen in shifts, one group of dancers breaking for lunch while the others rehearse on.

Of course, there's always an outside chance you could be finished by lunchtime but, assuming you're required in the afternoon, you're likely to have a break in the middle of the day of perhaps an hour, or an hour and a half. Aside from the time out between afternoon rehearsals and evening performance – a break more accurately known as 'getting ready for the show' – it's the only real hiatus in the working day.

It's into this hour that the non-dancing elements of a dancer's life must be shoehorned: costume fittings, preparing shoes, physiotherapy, body conditioning, massage, video study (to learn a new role), chiropody and more. It's also the hour in which you can make contact with the world outside: phone calls, emails, appointments with dentists, banks, shopping, haircuts, house purchasing, marriage preparations or divorce. In the 1980s, we did all these things without mobile phones and the Internet and, while technology might have made some of this easier, I suspect this isn't the case. People just want an answer faster these days.

And on top of this, there's eating.

Dancers need to eat. That much is obvious. The challenge is when, what and how much. A dancer's schedule doesn't necessarily align with the digestive system. Food takes around four hours to pass through the system and into the small intestine but a dancer doesn't usually have four hours to digest a meal in the middle of the day. Dancing on a full stomach is not only uncomfortable, it's ill advised too. After you eat, blood is diverted to the stomach to aid with the process of digestion, which means there is less available to supply the brain and the working muscles. If there's less blood, there's also less oxygen, leading to sluggishness, a decrease in co-ordination and the risk of injury. There was logic to our parents' demands that we sit down for a while after a meal to 'let your food go down'.

The type of exercise dancers do, for the most part, is anaerobic – fast, short bursts of high intensity – and the only energy source that can fuel this kind of activity is carbohydrates: pasta, bread, potatoes, cereals, rice, fruit and sugar. Of course, you need a varied diet: proteins are the body's building blocks, essential for maintaining and repairing tissue; fats carry certain essential vitamins and are required for growth and for sexual reproduction; vitamins and minerals regulate body functions and help to form bones and teeth; and water is vital for transporting nutrients in and waste out, for regulating temperature and for lubricating joints and blood flow. Energy production is the result of a complicated interaction of all of these nutrients, but carbohydrates are especially important for dancers as they are the only nutrient that can be stored as glycogen, the fuel that muscles require in high-intensity exercise like dance.

So foods rich in carbohydrates are essential but they're also the kind that is slow to digest, the kind that can feel 'heavy' in your stomach or make you feel sleepy for a while. There is no chance of getting what you need in a dancing day, at least not all of it, at lunchtime. The most important time to eat, perhaps paradoxically, is the time you least feel like it: after the show. When the body's glycogen stores are emptied, through high-intensity exercise, they are much more receptive to new supplies: like a sponge that has dried out, they soak it all up.

Directly after curtain down, there is a window of between fifteen and sixty minutes in which you can take advantage of this biological fact and stock up for the next day, by eating a high-carbohydrate meal. Any sluggishness it might induce is not a problem: it can be slept off. Miss the window and your glycogen stores will only partially refill. After several days of failing to refuel effectively, you'll be pretty much dancing on empty.

If you finish the day with a good meal and start with a good breakfast, during the working day you can simply top yourself up, little and often, with easy-to-digest carbohydrate snacks and plenty of water: fruit, vegetables, energy drinks, cereal bars, yoghurt, sandwiches with low-fat fillings, a jacket potato if you have time. It's not exactly a gourmet diet, but then it's intended to satisfy your energy demands, not your taste buds.

It would be foolish to pretend that every dancer eats like this and that none of us has ever struggled with the delicate balance between energy in and energy out. Contemporary fashion and the culture of the ballet world combine to exert a tremendous pressure on the dancer to be lean. Modern choreography and costumes usually favour the lean, as do audiences, critics, dancers and often, although not always, company directors. Where there is pressure for extreme leanness, a dancer's discipline and single-mindedness often serves her far too effectively in achieving this. The dancer's daily focus on perfection, an extraordinary capacity for hard work and exceptional willpower are a powerful combination.

For many years (and in my case, at least half of my career) dancers struggled with this quest for the ideal physique in a confusion of unknowing, battling with fad diets and alternating famine and feast, with dubious dressing-room wisdom about the only source of information available. The dangers of this are both immediate and long-term. The undernourished dancer risks poor performance (through lack of energy), injury (through loss of the ability to concentrate and through weak muscles and bones) and illness or infection (through suppression of the immune system). In the longer term, a dancer who persistently consumes too little food can compromise bone health (leading to stress fractures and osteoporosis), the reproductive system, the kidneys and the heart.

Times have moved on since I started to dance: there is now good advice and support available and a better understanding of how best to nourish a body on which such extreme physical demands are made.

Give or take the odd stubborn resurgence of Atkins and its like, the protein myth has been exploded and dancers are not, for the most part, trying to get through the day on a diet of steak and eggs. Many, many dancers (and athletes) have proved that it is possible to be lean, yet healthy, in a demanding profession. Beauty need not be born of its own despair. There is no reason for any of us to be missing lunch.

Costume Fittings

After food, it's time for a costume fitting. Normally, the scheduler will try to avoid squeezing a fitting into a dancer's lunch break but sometimes it's the only place it can go. So you head directly from the canteen to the production wardrobe, to try on a new costume. It's the second fitting you've had and the costume hanging there waiting for you is now looking much more like it did in the designer's drawings. At first, it seemed to be mostly pins, chalk marks and plain cream calico. Now, it's close to something you can imagine wearing on the stage. You take off most of your clothes and prepare to stand around for a while as material is pulled up and pinned in, or seams snipped open and let out.

The wardrobe department keeps a detailed chart of measurements on file for each dancer: not only the basics, such as height, bust, waist and hips, but also the statistics of bits you never expected to be vital. They know the circumference of your head, the distance from the nape of your neck to your waist and then again to the floor, from wrist to elbow and elbow to shoulder, then shoulder to nape. They know the span of your arms and (my favourite) the distance from 'point to point' (between one nipple and the other). With all this knowledge, the costume-makers are able to create a first draft of your costume in advance of the first fitting, saving time in a schedule that's always packed.

Today, it's a dress, knee length, with a tightly fitted bodice and long sleeves. There's a multi-layered, brightly coloured underskirt below the embroidered top layer, adding to the already considerable weight. Most worrying though is the heavily flounced, asymmetric hemline: to the designer, it's the final flourish; to the dancers, it's a red flashing light. There are two problems here. First, the hemline and second, the flounces. When you turn in an asymmetric skirt it's a bit like the action of a hula hoop on your hips: the skirt whips around unevenly, pulling your centre from side to side and greatly reducing the speed and, therefore, the number of turns you can do. And the flounces add weight: as you turn, the skirt flies up and out, creating the effect of a dinner plate around the body. The weight of the flounces adds force to the outer edge of the plate, whereas what you really want is all the force to be gathered into your centre; this is what facilitates the turn.

You're not best pleased: the steps are hard enough, without adding handicaps. There are other dancers performing the role and each one of them has made the same points, all to no avail. The most that's been achieved, through combined lobbying, is a reduction in the number of underskirts beneath the problematical top layer. On the plus side, the bodice is fine: plenty of elasticity, so you can raise your arms, bend sideways and backwards and lift your leg in *arabesque*. And it is beautiful: sleek and elegant, with a scooped neckline and low-cut back. If it weren't for the skirt, you'd be delighted.

Even with its challenges, this dress, of body-hugging stretch velvet, is a lot easier to wear than the costumes of the last century. Costumes have changed enormously over the last hundred years, in design, in structure and in the materials from which they are made. Royal Opera House Collections have examples of costumes dating back to 1861, which make asymmetric skirts look like a gift. Before man-made fabrics, the only material with any kind of elasticity at all was knitted – cotton, silk or wool. It stretched, but it didn't retract and so everything was either wrinkled and baggy or stiff like a cardboard box. And unless costumes were made of silk, they were likely to be heavy, too. Costumes couldn't easily be washed, and so removable cotton pads were stitched into the armpits and removed, laundered and replaced between wearings and when the costume passed to another cast. With man-made fabrics – nylon and then Lycra – came a small revolution. Now, fabrics could cling to contours; they could stretch to allow movement and then return to their original shape; they could be light but appear heavy – and they could be washed, too.

Ballet costumes are very often works of art in their own right, the attention to detail and period accuracy astonishing. If a costume looks boned or laced, it almost certainly is. There will be authentic petticoats and bloomers, where the design demands it, and corsets and bustles, too. Each of these masterpieces bears close-up scrutiny and each is made to last. There are costumes worn on stage today at the Royal Opera House that were made for the very first performance, sometimes up to fifty years ago. This dress, like many of the costumes made for me (mere whippersnappers) will still be seen on the stage for a good few years yet.

The Shoe Room

With twenty minutes still in hand before the next rehearsal begins, there's time to drop in to the shoe room to pick up another batch of *pointe* shoes. The original shoe room at the Royal Opera House – at least the one I knew – was a basement cupboard in which Nesta, the shoe lady, had lived for as long as anyone could remember. Every dancer – then, as now – had an individual cubby hole, marked with her surname, which held a little pile of satin shoes, one of each pair tucked inside the other, as well as any other 'special' shoes required at the time: coloured shoes for particular ballets, heeled character shoes and canvas or leather 'flats'. Nesta's job was to keep each dancer supplied, with stocks in reserve, and to resolve any problems she might have with her shoes – the fit, the shape or the support.

Nowadays the shoe room is upstairs among the studios, just slightly bigger, and with a desk and a computer to allow today's shoe supervisor to track more efficiently the traffic of shoes in and out. But there is still the honeycomb wall of cubby holes, alphabetically arranged and packed tightly with shoes. It's one of the most frequently photographed locations in the Royal Opera House, combining as it does the romanticism of the ballet with the pragmatism of the dancer's life.

The earliest ballet dancers didn't have to contend with *pointe* shoes. They danced in soft slippers whose low heels limited the complexity and speed of movements. As technique advanced, the heels came off and then, during the eighteenth century, the idea of dancing on *pointe* was introduced. No one is quite sure which ballerina was the first, but there is a lovely description of Anna Heinel dancing on 'stilt-like tip toe' as early as 1770. In 1795, Charles Didelot invented a 'flying machine', which lifted dancers upwards so that they appeared to pause on their toes before they left the ground. Audiences loved it and from that point on, both dancers and choreographers began to explore new ways, without wires, to 'hover' between the ground and the air.

Poised to take flight, on the very tips of her toes, the balletic heroines of the period – *sylph* or *wili* – were the embodiment of the Romantic ideal, a perfect fit with the nineteenth-century obsession with death and otherworldliness. It wasn't long before dancing on *pointe* was all the rage, even though *pointe* shoes were still no more than leather-soled satin slippers, with toes padded and the sides and backs darned to increase support. The real strength – as it is now – was in the muscles of the feet and the legs.

Sometimes I wonder whether shoes have changed much in the intervening years. Compared to the custom-made, gold-leather, logo-embossed, no-request-too-difficult footwear of world-class athletes, *pointe* shoes remain remarkably low-tech, an ancient recipe of satin, hessian, glue and leather handed down through generations, each pair handmade and no two pairs ever identical. (In fact, even the notion of 'pairs' is misleading. A 'pair' of *pointe* shoes is, in reality, two identical shoes, without so much as a nod to the fact that our two feet are not carbon copies of each other.)

Most of us first started to dance on *pointe* aged around ten, after three years' consistent training. Some dancers start younger than this, but young skeletons are still in development and without sufficient maturity, technique and strength, *pointe* work can have damaging long-term effects. Like most of my classmates, I'd done a little *pointe* work before I arrived at White Lodge. My first *pointe* shoes (which I still have) came not from a specialist supplier, but from the now long-gone Crofts Department Store in Skegness High Street, from a general shoe department on the first floor.

I can see it now, the pine, sloped-top box on which the shoe rested as I slid my foot inside, the hard block of the toe and the rigid back, and the shop assistant holding my hands as I climbed on to *pointe* for the first time ever on the store's slippery carpet, surveying my feet in the curiously angled Lilliputian mirror particular to the selling of shoes. I'm sure she told me they looked perfect and I'm sure that to the next customer she was selling plimsolls, Clark's school lace-ups or bedroom slippers.

I took the shoes home proudly and wore them until I went to White Lodge where, in our first week, the professionals from Gamba arrived in a van filled with small pink satin shoes. Each of the twelve new arrivals was individually fitted and issued with two pairs of shoes and ribbons to match. The price was added to our parents' end-of-term bill. (More of those extras, which always seemed to add up to the same amount as the fees themselves.) We took the shoes away, to sleep with them under our pillows and to prepare them for class.

At White Lodge, we all darned our shoes: with thick pink thread and a wide-eyed needle, we would sit for long hours trying to create an armour of smooth, neat chain-stitching underneath the toes and around the blocked tip. In theory, this stitching lengthened the life of the shoe. It was also supposed to create a more effective platform on which to balance and to help guard against slipping. But we soon realised that darning was something only students did – and so promptly gave up on the practice. Professionals went through so many pairs of shoes every week that darning each one was an impossibility.

By the time you're dancing professionally, you're in a position to make certain demands about your shoes, choosing your favourite maker and specifying modifications – lower vamps, higher backs or a specially shaped 'wing' block. Some dancers even go along to the factory to discuss their needs in person (giving a whole new meaning to the phrase 'she's gone to meet her maker'). The shoes in your particular slot in the honeycomb wall – each pair crafted exactly to your specifications and leaving the factory with your name already marked on their soles – are, in some small way, a testament to the fact that you made it as a dancer. Even so, the visit to the shoe room has nothing of the thrill of that trip to Crofts, or of the arrival of the Gamba van for the first time at White Lodge.

The trip to the shoe room is a weekly occurrence at least. With nothing more than a quick glance to check for unwanted ridges around the block, or any irregularities in the shape at the front, four pairs this time are logged out and taken away. Later, they'll be subject to a thorough examination before any effort is invested in them, on attaching ribbons or breaking them in. For now, it's time to get back to the studios. Ten more minutes before the afternoon rehearsals begin.

Injury

On the way to the studio, you might just pop into the physiotherapy suite to book an appointment for tomorrow. The room is invariably full and the physio-therapists busy: there are injured dancers to treat and tired dancers to support with a range of preventative therapies including massage, manipulation, stretch-ing and strengthening exercises. Just outside the door, last night's principal is going full pelt on the ellipti-cal cross-trainer and in a room alongside two or three dancers are working with intense concentration on the body-conditioning equipment. These are dancers on a break.

Aside from annual holidays (taken as a compulsory block each summer) and one day off a week, the only hiatus in a dancer's working life is when it's enforced by injury. Working at these levels of intensity, it's almost inevitable that dancers will endure at least one period of lay-off, through injury, during a performing career.

Leaving aside the almost limitless parts of the body to which injury can occur, there are really only two types of injury: traumatic and chronic (or overuse). Traumatic is the kind that happens instantly, through accident: breaking a bone or rupturing a tendon on an unstable landing from a jump, for example. It's usually impossible to carry on walking, let alone dancing, when a bone or tendon actually breaks and so the dancer has no choice but to bow to the inevitable.

Chronic injuries, on the other hand, are the sort that build up over time, through repeated stress to one particular part of the body. Tendonitis is a typical chronic condition, in which microscopic tears, from overuse, cause the tendon to swell and stiffen in an attempt to force the dancer to stop. Unfortunately, this self-defence mechanism is not always effective, because although dancing with a chronic injury is extremely painful, it *is* possible. A very long warm-up will eventually ease the stiffness and anti-inflammatories will reduce the swelling and increase the range of movement possible. This is why dancers can continue for months, sometimes years, on chronic injuries. I know, because I did.

Determined not to miss any rehearsals for my first *Swan Lake*, I refused to stop to allow an Achilles tendonitis to recover. If I'd caught it immediately, I might have needed a week or so out, with another week to work my way back to full strength. Instead, I danced on and on, through the autumn *Swan Lakes* and still on, into the spring. Eventually the tendonitis was so severe, immune to painkillers and resistant to warm-up, that I was forced, finally, to take the injury seriously instead of trying to pretend it might just go away on its own. It was six months before I was ready to go back to work, after treatment from the company physiotherapists and, most importantly in this kind of injury, the rest my body required in order for it to heal.

As soon as the recovery is under way, you can begin the process of finding out why the injury happened in the first place. Unless there is an inherent structural weakness (possible, but unlikely in a dancer who has reached professional status) the cause can usually be found in a technical fault, something that might have developed through bad habits, extreme fatigue or even poor teaching. In coaching classes, perhaps one on one, you start to explore the basis of the fault with a specialist teacher.

It usually makes sense to start by looking above the site of the injury to uncover its cause. For instance, if the hips are slightly twisted because the muscles on one side of the back are stronger than the other, the muscles in the thigh will be pulling unevenly to compensate, which will, in turn, impact on the alignment of the knee. So while the actual injury might be experienced in the knee, the source of the problem is the imbalance in the back.

Slowly, over several weeks, you'll work on correcting the fault, establishing new movement patterns and regaining your strength. These sessions are both frustrating – because the process is always slower than you'd like it to be – and fascinating, because they allow you to approach a technique you learned as a child with the insights of an adult. It's amazing how often dancers finally understand a movement that has perplexed them for years through the process of recovering from injury.

Given the brevity of a dancer's career, a career in which roles come along only every so often and the next generation is always right there behind you, perhaps it's not surprising that we are so unwilling to give in to injury. When we do finally wave the white flag, we're faced with a day without routine – no class, no rehearsals and no performances – and a chance, perhaps for the first time, to concentrate on something other than dancing.

Recovering from my first injury, post-*Swan Lake*, I struggled to know what to do with myself. Rehabilitation techniques were not quite so advanced back then and, while I was receiving good treatment, there was no suggestion that I should take up any kind of alternative exercise in order to retain my fitness. No more than half an inch of tissue in my Achilles tendon was injured, but the entire 5 feet 6 inches of me put my feet up. I went round in a daze, acutely aware of what I was missing out on and desperate to get back to work.

Several years later, a second injury and a minor operation took me out for another extended period of time. This time I knew much more about my body and about exercise physiology and I came back fitter than I had been when the injury forced me to stop. I also seized the opportunity I'd missed the last time around to focus my energies on interests beyond the ballet world.

Many years later, I heard the Japanese ballerina Miyako Yoshida talking to a distraught young student who had just learned she was suffering from a stress fracture that would recover only with prolonged rest. She advised the young girl to treat the injury as a gift: a rare period in a dancer's life when you need not be permanently exhausted and overworked, and when you can turn your attention to those things which, in a busy career, you never seem to be able to find time to explore.

This summed up how I had approached my second time out from dancing. The realisation that this time I found the lay off not bewildering but stimulating, exciting and satisfying, disarmed, at last, my fear that I would never find anything that I would enjoy the way I enjoyed dancing. I came back from the injury to dance for three or four years more but, looking back, it's clear that this revelation marked the beginning of the end of my first career.

2.30 – 4.00 Soloist and Principal Calls

Post-lunch, and the atmosphere in the studio now is different from the atmosphere at 12 noon. There are ten minutes to go before the rehearsal begins and a dancer sits alone in the shadow of the *barre*, choosing between the comfort of old shoes and the possibility of breaking in a new pair. She's wearing pink tights, cut off at the ankles, a leotard and a practice tutu – the stiff net skirt only, unadorned on its calico basque and recycled for use in the studio from an old costume that was on its way out. It creates a pool of tulle around her from which her legs extend sideways, one east and one west.

Her hair is bunched thoughtlessly into an elastic band at the nape of her neck, more dog's tail, post-docking, than pony tail. The ends of her woollen leg warmers have unravelled and formed a tangled spaghetti of pink thread around her ankles. New shoe in hand, with practised expertise she digs the blade of a pair of scissors into its inner sole to pull out a tiny nail, then fractures its rigidity in an exact spot, unique to her, before banging it mercilessly on the corner of an iron stage weight lying near by.

A few minutes ahead of time, the pianist arrives. There may or may not be a brief chat about the rehearsal, the day, the role, or life in general before the *répétiteur* sweeps in, driven still by the energy from the rehearsal she has just left. 'What would you like to do today? Do you want to run through all your solos to build up stamina? Or shall we work on them section by section?' Aside from the more obvious distinction (the number of people in the room) this conversation, this introduction of shared responsibility into the preparation for performance, always seemed to me the most marked difference between this principal call and the *corps de ballet* rehearsals of earlier years.

It took me some eleven years to reach the longed-for position of principal dancer with The Royal Ballet. This slow train to the top is not typical, but neither is it unique. Progression up through the ranks is entirely down to the discretion of the company director and so it's influenced not only by individual progress but by factors over which a dancer has no power at all: casting, available repertoire, injuries (your own, and those of others), luck and, perhaps above all, taste.

To reach the rank of principal, you generally need to have several leading roles already within your repertoire, danced while still officially at soloist level. But if a company is blessed with top-level talent, the director's first challenge will be to share the available roles between the pool of existing principals, in a five loaves and two fishes exercise, and never mind the soloists waiting for a lucky break. Injury can curtail chances or open up unexpected opportunities, depending on whether it happens to you or to someone above you on the cast sheet. And then there is the question of taste, which is hard to define and even harder to overcome. A director can have nothing but admiration for a dancer's skill, dedication, intelligence and resilience but, in the end, if she doesn't fire the imagination in same the way as another dancer, who may appear less obviously accomplished or less dedicated, the director won't be able to give her the roles she feels she deserves. As I learned early on: sometimes you're cast; sometimes you're not.

Rehearsing Solo

Typically, dancers climb their way out of the *corps* via the short solos in the classics – the Prologue Fairies in *Sleeping Beauty*, or the first act *pas de trois* in *Swan Lake*. These solos are small and perfectly formed, rarely lasting more than two or three minutes, and so rehearsals can be correspondingly short: perhaps half an hour for a single dancer or an hour if a group of dancers is called at the same time. The run of rehearsals normally begins with this kind of group call, for general recapping, and so the first solo rehearsal a dancer experiences is often not truly alone, but with the four or five other dancers who will perform the variation over a series of perhaps ten performances.

There is a natural hierarchy in these calls, based on the order of casting, which usually relates to the seniority of the dancers involved. First cast and the more senior dancers will work at the front, with the newest cast and covers towards the back of the studio, keen to be noticed but equally intent on not getting in the way of the soloists up front.

As a general rule, these classical solos are made up of four or five sequences of movement, each of which takes place in a different location on the stage – perhaps centre, downstage left, upstage right and then finishing with an obligatory diagonal of turning steps from the left-hand upstage corner to the downstage right. Generally, the *répétiteur* can assume the dancers know the steps: they will have been learned first at school, in weekly solo classes, and then reinforced through years of observation, either from the wings or from the perspective of a Court Lady, Lilac Attendant, or Peasant, dressing the sides of the stage while others do the dancing.

With no need to teach the steps, or even do much in the way of a recap, the rehearsal starts with a run-through of the solo, which serves both to refresh the dancers' memories and to give an idea of the work required to bring it up to scratch. The *répétiteur* will then break down each section in detail, offering corrections on the choreography, the technique or the style. A dancer might be taking the arms through fifth *en avant* to *arabesque*, rather than directly from fifth *en bas*; she might be dropping her supporting knee inwards on the landing from a jump; or the dynamic might be too soft, when the solo requires a crisper approach. Sections are tried again with the music and then, finally, the whole solo, now greatly improved, is put together and rehearsed, one dancer at a time.

If you're a cover rather than cast, your moment may come at the end of this type of rehearsal, with just a few minutes to spare. 'Bull, why don't you have a go?' was the prelude to my first ever solo rehearsal with The Royal Ballet. So the first essay at dancing alone is often in front of the most frightening audience there is: the soloists already cast in the variation, who may or may not think adding you to the list was a good idea.

While the other dancers have been thoroughly scrutinised (a process some *répétiteurs* like to call 'cleaning'), you have been carefully noting every last correction, even those that were not necessarily relevant to your particular strengths and style. Summoned to 'have a go', you gather up your courage and all those yet-to-be-absorbed corrections and head to the upstage left corner of the studio, heart pounding and adrenalin whitewashing your nerve endings, to try your luck. 'Don't worry, we'll all applaud,' one of those glamorous soloists whispered as I passed.

Dancing the Lead

At some point, if you're destined for the top, you find your name right at the beginning of a cast sheet, listed alongside the leading role. This can happen at any point in your career: at least in The Royal Ballet the ranking system does not prevent dancers from being cast above their official level and it's normal to see a mixture of principals, soloists and even talented *corps de ballet* dancers cast in, or covering, principal roles. Frequently, the roles – and the order in which you dance them as you ascend through the ranks – have no more than a haphazard logic. It was several years before I graduated out of the *corps* in the big, classical ballets. In the meantime, I'd danced my first ever solo in a twentieth-century ballet, as well as 'second principal' – Lescaut's Mistress – in Kenneth Mac-Millan's *Manon*. It's a notoriously demanding role, technically, but the hardest thing for me – an unsure twenty-two-year-old, desperate not to make a fool of herself – was the requirement to flirt with the 'Dancing Gents', most of whom were established company soloists with whom I'd exchanged not a single word.

Rehearsals can start anything up to two or three months in advance of your first performance, depending on the role, its length and the level of challenge and complexity it entails. Because the principals are working flat out most of the time, they retain a high level of base fitness to which role-specific strengths and skills can be added relatively efficiently – if you keep the pot simmering it's so much easier to bring it to the boil. And so, with perhaps five or six weeks to go before your big night, a series of solo and *pas de deux* rehearsals appears on the call sheet and you find yourself alone in the studio, sitting under the *barre*, wondering which shoes to wear. It's the beginning of a process of which the audience sees but the smallest part: the last two or three hours of some thirty, forty or fifty spent working on each role.

Rehearsal is a richly rewarding time, an intense period of exploration and research. You might expect dancers to prefer performing to rehearsing – surely it's 'the real thing'? – but some dancers, if pushed, would admit that rehearsals are where they feel most alive. The studio, for me, is the place where the true analysis takes place, the real forensic investigation of a role and the technique it requires. It's where a myriad of options can be tested and explored. In performance, the dancer is obliged to narrow down those options, to pick just one for presentation to the paying audience. This public trial is the final (and most important) component of the process: it's the dancer's version of product testing in the market place and it either confirms your assumptions or, in the worst case, sends you right back to the drawing board to work out a different approach.

Over the course of a career, if life were fair, a dancer would have the chance to try out a vast range of interpretations, new approaches and different techniques in performance, but it's not, and we don't. Depending on those hard-to-influence factors (casting, repertoire, injuries, luck and taste) you may find yourself dancing only a handful of *Swan Lakes* and a hat trick of

Sleeping Beauties in twenty years. So perhaps it makes sense that some dancers prefer the studio, where they can dance these roles endlessly and in as many ways as they can imagine.

There's one more notable difference between studio and stage: in the studio, it really doesn't matter if things go wrong. In fact it's essential: failure is an important component of learning – it's the brain's teacher – and besides, if you don't fail from time to time you're probably not trying hard enough. In the studio, where the consequences of failure are only positive, you're free to take risks, in every sense: physical, emotional, dramatic. But in attempting to transfer the bravery possible in the studio to the one-off performance on stage, the dancer fights a complex psychological battle. We understand, intellectually, that when physical challenge is involved, the more cautious you are, the less likely you are to succeed. Try throwing a dart with any degree of hesitation and you'll see what I mean. It's unlikely to reach the board, let alone hit bull's-eye. Where technique is concerned, she who hesitates is, indeed, lost. Learning to trust that knowledge can be an ever present challenge, at least for some of us, and the temptation to 'play it safe' sometimes wins out.

The dancers I most admire are the ones who are able to carry with them into performance the bravery of their approach in the studio. These are the dancers who never, ever undercut a movement, who never shrink on stage from the version they have prepared in rehearsal. They never play it safe and the results are breathtaking, astounding and glorious.

Handing on the Heritage

The classics are such a regular feature of the repertoire that they form part of a company's DNA. They might not be performed every season, but it's rare that more than a year or two goes by without a *Swan Lake*, a *Beauty* or a *Nutcracker* in the schedule. What this means is that as we climb up through the ranks, from Court Lady or Peasant to Bluebird or *pas de trois*, we are all the time watching and absorbing the roles we might, if we're lucky, dance next. By the time – if – we get our chance, we know the ballets from start to finish.

This might not be as true now as it once was: ballet companies are more diverse than ever before, with dancers joining from a variety of different schools and countries: the version of the classics they have absorbed through their training might not be quite the same as the version they're required to perform.

With no – or few – steps to learn, the rehearsals are all about finding your way into a role that has, in some cases, been one of the benchmarks by which a ballerina is judged for over a hundred years. It's easy to be awed by this sense of heritage and history, never truly convinced that we have the right to be performing the same steps Svetlana Beriosova, Margot Fonteyn or Monica Mason so movingly inhabited. The *répétiteur* for these principal rehearsals might well be a dancer of exactly this stature, someone who excelled in the part and can pass on an abundance of practical wisdom along with the choreographic text: how to pace rehearsals, how to choose the right shoes, how to ensure your headdress stays on during the *fouettés*, how to deal with difficult partners or unfavourable reviews.

Crucially, that former dancer will be able to pass on a deep first-hand knowledge, gleaned through performing the role, as well as the knowledge handed down during her own rehearsals from a dancer of the generation before. This passing on of the repertoire, from one dancer to another, connects today's dancers with their artistic heritage on a daily basis and, in some cases, there is an unbroken thread stretching back to the very first performances: Darcey Bussell was taught *The Firebird* by Monica Mason, who learned from Margot Fonteyn, who was coached by Tamara Karsavina, the ballerina for whom the role was created in 1910.

The challenge, within this system, is to find one's own interpretation, one's own validity, when such a roster of stars has already made a mark on the role. You can search and search for the key to the character, the thing that brings it alive in your imagination, the personal link that makes it real but, for some ballets, it never comes. At other times, it reveals itself in unexpected places. I remember Natalia Makarova describing how she found her Aurora in the innocent face of a young ballet fan who visited her backstage after a performance of *Sleeping Beauty*.

I unexpectedly found a way into Odette's character through a line from *The Killing Fields*, spoken by Dith Pran to Sydney Schanberg when they met again, many years after the war in Vietnam ended. In the fourth act of *Swan Lake*, Odette shows a capacity for boundless clemency when the Prince betrays her, unwittingly, by swearing his love for Odile. Stumbling through the flock of swans he falls to his knees, head bowed, at her feet. She gently lifts his chin so that he can look into her eyes and see what she feels. 'Nothing to forgive. Nothing to forgive.'

The *répétiteur* fulfils a different role in these principal calls from the part he or she plays with the *corps*: it's less about marshalling forces and imparting information than about bringing out the best performance the artist can find within. A skilled *répétiteur*, coaching a principal role, passes on all the wise counsel and good sense acquired over her own career, but leaves open the possibility that new generations are likely to see the world differently and may have something of their own to add. Feedback is given, but often in a discursive fashion – suggestions and ideas rather than corrections to rectify mistakes.

With the best *répétiteurs*, the guidance is so pertinent that it forms a kind of on-board route map, a dancer's personal satnav; something that can be turned to in performance to get you back on track when things don't go according to plan. Through this kind of clever and constructive coaching, the steps, the style and the musicality of each sequence fuse together, so that paying attention to any one of these elements immediately triggers attention to the next. And this makes sense: on stage, you want the steps to happen automatically so that your conscious brain is freed up to concentrate on bringing the character alive and responding to the people around you.

There are other ways to work, of course, and they all have their place. Some *répétiteurs* like to call out helpful hints as the dancer is running through the solo, willing her to stay on balance, turn out, or jump higher. 'Up, up' or 'hold, hold, hold' sing out above the music's melody. There is logic to this – a dancer can begin to associate the guidance with the steps, creating an in-built help menu – but a risk, too, in that attention is diverted from doing the step to listening to and attempting to apply the correction.

There is also the 'do it again' type of *répétiteur*. 'No, that's wrong, do it again' would come the advice after a failed balance or a dodgy *pirouette*. The illogic of this struck me only years later. Why would you want to do it again, if it was wrong? If it's wrong, you probably need to stop and think before trying a different approach. If it works, *then* do it again. And again. And again. Practice makes perfect. It's a cliché because it's true.

Partners

Later on in the day, perhaps immediately after this one, you might have a rehearsal with your partner to go through the *pas de deux*. It's likely to involve a different *répétiteur*: more often than not, *pas de deux* rehearsals are taken by a man, rather than a woman, because although a *pas de deux* is a dance for two, the specific skills of partnering (rather than 'being partnered' – the easier of the two options) are definitely the domain of the male.

Young, male dancers are judged to be ready to begin to learn partnering skills round about the age of fifteen. At White Lodge, as in company life, the daily ballet classes were always single-sex – one for the young women and one for the young men – and so it was a strange sensation, that first *pas de deux* class, when the two sexes were together in the same studio for perhaps the first time, eyeing each other across the room and wondering (given that there are always more women than men) who was going to be left out.

Like adolescents at a prom, the males looked mostly at the floor while we females giggled and blushed and hoped we'd end up with the big strapping guys who'd be sure to be able to lift us up. The teacher swiftly grouped us into trios (two women for every man – some kind of adolescent fantasy) to ensure that each of us would have an appropriately sized partner with whom we could work, one after the other, in turns.

It all starts simply, with supported partnering rather than the more taxing lifts: *promenades*, in which the female stands in a single position, on *pointe*, and the male rotates her around her supporting leg by holding either her waist or her hand. (The balances at the end of the famous Rose Adagio in *Sleeping Beauty* are each preceded by a *promenade* in *attitude* supported by a single hand.) These simple techniques allow both the dancers to begin to understand the dynamics of working together, where the point of balance is for a woman on *pointe*, what happens to the body weight when the rotation begins, how a very slight movement in one dancer impacts on the other. It's like very early courtship, testing out how it feels to be a couple rather than going it alone.

Simple lifts come next, *temps levés* in *arabesque* or *jetés*, lifts in which the female's jump helps to add upward thrust, and then perhaps the most straightforward of 'dead' lifts, where there is no jump and the male is on his own. The class then moves on to supported *pirouettes*, and while the male has to learn the specialised technique of 'flicking' the dancer's hips and then providing a frame with his hands in which she can turn, the female dancer has to learn the difference between the force she needs to turn on her own and the reduction in force required when she has a partner for support.

The more flamboyant and acrobatic overhead lifts come a year or even two later. Lifting another person above your head and getting her safely back down again puts tremendous pressure on the spine and the knees – however light she may be – and it can't be attempted until the male student has gained sufficient maturity and strength.

Dancers cast in principal roles will have mastered all of these basic partnering skills way back, at school and in their early years in the company. Here, in rehearsal at principal level, the task for the *répétiteur* is to help the dancers negotiate the particular challenges of the ballet's choreography – its unusual lifts or off-balance manoeuvres – and to smooth out any rough edges between them so that these two dancers – applauded and promoted for their individual achievements - can dance effectively as one.

Audiences love a couple. Think Fonteyn and Nureyev, Fred and Ginger, Bogart and Bacall, Torvill and Dean. It's not just a ballet thing: there is nothing we like better than to imagine that the passion of a partnership extends beyond stage or screen. The truth is slightly more prosaic. Dancing together as a couple is probably easier if the day-to-day banalities of cohabitation aren't a simmering subtext: it's hard to act out Romeo and Juliet's innocent ardour when there's an unresolved issue over the toothpaste cap.

There's no denying that audiences in the know read a special intensity into the stage partnerships of offstage couples, but it's impossible to prove this exists as there is no possibility of comparing it with its opposite – the same pair of dancers, but as 'just good friends'.

It's certainly true that some of the most successful dance partnerships were not an offstage couple – Sibley and Dowell, for instance. So if it isn't real-life passion, what is it? Is it possible to analyse the alchemy that raises some partnerships above others? There are clearly some factors that work for (and, in their absence, against) partnerships: physical compatibility, a similar response to music and a complementary approach to the working process are some of the most obvious. But just as some successful marriages can't, with logic, be explained, so some partnerships work out against all the odds.

On paper, ballet's most famous partnership, Fonteyn and Nureyev, might not have looked very hopeful. Photographs show that he was relatively short and slim as a reed while Fonteyn, on *pointe*, was clearly taller than him and pleasantly feminine in her curves. What's more, she was forty-two and on the verge of retirement when the twenty-three-year-old Russian left the Soviet Union to make his home in the West. She was polite and well mannered, very proper and self-effacing. He, by all accounts, was fiery and temperamental, focused, for the most part, on himself.

At White Lodge, our weekly History of Ballet lessons – more a series of fascinating anecdotes than a structured course – would often include stories from Fonteyn and Nureyev rehearsals. The one that has stayed with me tells how he dragged her roughly along the floor in front of the entire company, expletives flying, when a sequence went wrong. Perfectly polite, Fonteyn examined the mark this left on her tights and said, calmly, 'Well, it won't wash off.'

A lasting partnership could not have seemed less likely, yet they became the benchmark by which all future couples would be judged.

During my years with The Royal Ballet, long-term partnerships had fallen out of vogue. Polygamy was the order of the day, and we were cast with a range of different partners, depending on the repertoire. There were fewer options for the taller women – while a few centimetres of difference doesn't matter, towering over your partner is a problem – but female dancers of average height could be allocated to almost any of the principal males. (I stopped counting my partners for *La Bayadère* when I'd clocked up twenty.)

There are advantages to both the promiscuous and permanent approach to partnerships. Variety brings new energy, new ideas, challenges and stimulation to roles you may think you've already mastered, but it does mean you have to start again with some basics, and articulate afresh likes and dislikes, on both sides. Working with a regular partner offers a shortcut to the substance of the rehearsal. There is no need to explain or explore the idiosyncrasies of your particular physique, musicality, style and approach and you can get straight down to work on the role in question.

When the audience sees a couple performing together, they are sharing in a mere three hours of what is, effectively, a full-time relationship. Over the course of the rehearsal period, you'll have got to know each other almost as intimately as you'll ever know anyone: your bodies, your rhythms, your moods, your fears and insecurities, what you eat and what you don't eat, what makes you laugh and what makes you cry.

You'll have seen each other at your most vulnerable: searching for the ultimate interpretation of a role involves trying out all sorts of routes, some of which inevitably lead to a dead end. You need to know that your partner is willing to go along with you, to join in and, when the dead end is a disaster, to laugh only when he's sure you're ready to think it's funny too.

As with any relationship, there has to be a good deal of give and take to make it work. A partnership is rarely a marriage of equals. Technique, dedication, musicality and artistry can all be on a par, but when conflicts of opinion arise, as they must, one of the pair will have to compromise, in an implied agreement to differ. In the end, most couples, long or short term, will settle into an unspoken hierarchy (often, but not always, based on seniority) and dancers get used to switching the role they take according to the casting.

The first rehearsals together are often sketchy and workmanlike, as the dancers walk through each section remembering the steps, the music and where and when they come on and off stage. The *répétiteur* may be joined by a notator, armed as ever with the choreographic score, and together they will map out the architecture of the ballet, teasing it back in full from steps half recalled. This part of the rehearsal process bears the same resemblance to performance as goats do to cashmere: it's hard to imagine how one turns into the other yet, without it, the end product wouldn't exist. But it doesn't take long to reconstruct the choreography and the pace of rehearsals soon picks up.

Each session begins with a quick discussion about which bit of the ballet needs the most attention and then the piano strikes up and the *répétiteur* sits back to watch. It won't be long, though, before a *pirouette* goes off or a lift goes wrong and proceedings are interrupted. The music stops and there is a chorus of 'sorry, sorry' as the dancers fall over themselves to be the first to apologise for the mishap. Dancers are generally over-critical of their failings and often prefer to shoulder the blame than to reproach their partner for his or her shortcomings.

As rehearsals progress towards the first night, there are good days, when it feels like flying, and bad days, when nothing will go right. When things go disastrously (the time, for instance, when I was dropped to the ground from a height of about seven feet) it's important to remember that your partner almost certainly feels worse about it than you do, with both ego and nerves as bruised as whichever bit of you it was that hit the ground first. On these occasions, it's best to adopt the 'falling off a bike' strategy. Get straight back on.

Dancers are usually pragmatic and professional about their working relationships: although they are bound to have favourites, they will always try to make each partnership as effective and enjoyable as possible. But it's hard to deny that seeing your name cast alongside some partners is like being handed a golden ticket. You know there will be no clash of egos and you can relax about the technical challenges of the various duets, safe in the knowledge that you are in expert and generous hands.

I was cast with Jonathan Cope for a handful of *Swan Lakes* on tour in America and those performances are among my happiest dancing memories. I was able to release my own internal safety catch and take new risks because I knew that he was behind me, steady, sure, and committed to making the *pas de deux* work for me, whatever it took. Without the need to focus 20 per cent of my attention behind me, I could dance out in a way I'd never experienced before.

Full Calls

All the work that has gone on in the separate principal, soloist and *corps de ballet* rehearsals comes together in the full calls. The studio is packed and the floor is set in a mock-up of the stage. At the front of the studio sits a line-up of *répétiteurs*, one responsible for the *corps*, one for the soloists and one for the principals. The baton is passed back and forth between them as the rehearsal progresses, each one protective of the group of dancers for which he is responsible and conscious of what they most need to get out of the call.

Many of the big classical ballets open with the *corps de ballet* on stage and so the ballet master kicks off. The tone is workaday, humorous, not at all precious, with corrections called out across and above the music: 'Lines . . . and one and two . . . Head to the right, please.' The soloists are likely to have their moment next and their *répétiteur* steps up. There is a subtle shift in mood: the hum around the room reduces a little, corrections are withheld until after the solo has finished, and there's a moment or two to go back and try again. The rehearsal moves on with another *corps de ballet* section ('Arms out on two, please . . . Accent up, and up . . . That's right') before it's time for the principals' first entrance. The *corps de ballet* exits and finds a place to sit or stand around the sides of the room. There's at least ten minutes before they're back on again. The centre of the studio is clear. The hum disappears to nothing now and all eyes are focused on the two dancers who are about to make their entrance.

For the principals, these studio calls can feel far more exposed than the stage, where costume, artifice and the proscenium arch offer, strangely, some sort of protection. A full call may be the first time you have ever tried to run the whole ballet in front of anyone other than the now familiar *répétiteurs*, and the dancers around you, at the edges of the studio, are perhaps the most knowledgeable and expert audience you will ever experience. It's no wonder some dancers prefer to do without a full call and risk, instead, their first try-out on the stage.

My abiding memory of studio full calls is of a moment exactly like this: I'm poised in the upstage corner – teasingly close to the exit door – preparing to run to the centre of the studio and I'm acutely aware of the entire company looking my way, their eyes a series of question marks. It was the final full call I ever danced. We were rehearsing a gala – *A Knight to Remember* – to mark Sir Anthony Dowell's retirement as company director and the fourth movement of *Symphony in C* had been chosen as the show's finale.

I had danced the lead role in this movement when the ballet first came into the repertoire in 1991, well suited, at the time, to its sharply defined, fast-paced *pirouettes*. This was some ten years later. I had told no one I was *also* leaving at the end of a season in which I had barely performed: two *Swan Lakes* (in November and December) and this single appearance the following May.

The solo that opens the fourth movement is akin to being shot out of a cannon: nought to sixty in no time at all, abrupt, frightening and a shock to the system. As the pianist let loose on Bizet's score and I ran on, I had the sense that everyone, including me, was genuinely intrigued to see whether or not I could still get up on to *pointe*, let alone get through it. I did, and I did the performance, but I doubt it was my finest hour. The only award it might have merited would have been for bravery.

4.00 – 5.30 New Work

There's a new mood again – an air of anticipation this time – in the studio as the dancers gather for the 4 o'clock call. A small group, perhaps two or three, huddles together in a comfort zone towards the back of the room, nerves disguised as bright and brittle energy. The choreographer arrives and lands bags, books and a coffee mug on a collection of upright chairs centre front, backed up tightly against the *barre*. The notator is already in place, on a seat to one side, sharpening a pencil in preparation to record the first move. At the grand piano, just inside the studio's door, the pianist flicks nervously through an unfamiliar score.

The dancers may be nervous, but they're thrilled to have been chosen to be a part of this new work. Having a role created around you and your particular qualities is, to quote Royal Ballet director Monica Mason, the difference between *prêt-à-porter* and *couture* – it's just a better fit. Choreographers creating a new work are usually given free rein to choose their cast from among the entire company and so, in a large company of talented dancers, it's always gratifying to be singled out.

Choreographers coming in from outside will see the dancers with fresh eyes and may give a younger artist her first chance. Those from within, particularly as they start their choreographic career, will have first-hand knowledge of the dancers as colleagues and friends and may pick an artist for a quality that has, until that point, gone unnoticed in the normal repertoire. Some choreographers will favour a particular type of dancer – strong and athletic or soft and lyrical – while others, depending on the work, may be looking for dramatic presence or innocent charm. Generally, though, choreographers are creative artists, intent on breaking new ground, and they are looking for dancers who are not afraid to be different.

It took me a good few years to work this out because it was in direct contradiction to the prevailing wisdom of the ballet world during my training: 'Work hard, stay in line, and you'll do well.' Some time after we had both retired, the American ballerina Cynthia Harvey and I discovered we had shared the same sense of betrayal when this truth finally dawned on us.

For the dancers, this first rehearsal is the first step on the journey to the opening night. For the choreographer, it's just another milestone along the way. Indeed, making the steps may even be the most straightforward part of the job. First, he's come up with an original idea and secured a commission – a sequence of events that is often reversed: companies can approach a choreographer with a request to make a new work or a choreographer can approach a company, producer, or venue with an idea that will then be commissioned and produced, sometimes in collaboration with other venues or producers. Next, he's put together a creative team.

The choreographer of a ballet fulfils all the tasks that would, in musicals or the theatre, be undertaken by the director: selecting the designer, lighting designer and music or, if it's specially written, the composer. He has determined the structure of the work, deciding on scale, duration and cast. And by the time rehearsals start, he has the outline of the production clearly in mind: where solos, duets and ensemble pieces happen, when characters make their entrances and exits, how the story, if there is one, will unfold. Designs are already under way. It's like a dot-to-dot puzzle, with the choreography the pencil line that joins it all up to reveal, by the dress rehearsal, the ballet as a complete picture.

As the clock edges towards the hour, the dancers are thinking not of this long trail of events that has brought them all together, but about the thrill of being involved and the possibility (whisper it quietly) that this could be the big break. And so we breathe in this nervous excitement, marking time on our respective sides of the studio as the possibility of a masterpiece hovers in the void between us. At 4 o'clock, we step into that void and the rehearsal begins.

From the Top

'Philip, can you play from the top, please?' With that brief request, the rehearsal begins. The choreographer sits still and listens intently while I try to pin down the music's asymmetric rhythms and identify tonal signposts to speed the process of inhabiting this unfamiliar musical landscape. A handful of bars later, Philip is interrupted, either by a clap of the hands, or a 'thank you' projected over the piano's harsh reduction of the composer's full score.

The choreographer stands up. 'You're going to come on from upstage left. I want you to rush on and pause in fifth position and then . . . Can you *jeté* and land on *pointe*?' It's not a conventional request, so I try a version of what I think he means. 'Other arm forwards . . . I want more shoulder. That's right. Can you do three of those? Then I want you to get to the other corner to start again from the other side. Fall back into *tendu*. Do that again. Now *soutenu* – in counts of three. That's right. OK, Philip, once again with Deborah.'

A first try dissolves into laughter all round as it's clear that there isn't enough time to fit in all the steps and reach the other corner to start again with the music. We find a compromise by shaving a few steps from the sequence. The notator writes down and rubs out and Philip clarifies the uneven bars: 'It's an eight, a four and a nine. Next time the tune comes back there's an extra two counts on the end.' Second time, it works and we're all happy.

And so we progress: a choreographer past his dancing days with a dancer eager and willing to give things a try on his behalf. Conversation is spare. Words are employed, for the most part, to describe not movements but feelings, intentions or relationships: 'You're disdainful . . . jealous . . . You're in charge here . . . I want you to feel as if . . .' From time to time, when verbal instructions don't achieve the intended effect, he will get up off his chair and manipulate my head, arm or leg until he finds what he's after.

Behind me, the second-cast dancer plugs away, keen to try out the steps but careful not to get in the way. Some of my idiosyncrasies – the *jetés* on to *pointe* - come back, but *en tournant*, earning an audible grimace from the back of the room. In these early rehearsals, the choreographer is focused, by and large, on the first cast: for roles like this one (a solo, rather than the principal character) it will be the notator and the *répétiteur*'s responsibility, further down the line, to ensure that the second cast knows the steps and is ready to go on.

Within ninety minutes, we've completed the minute-long variation and we run it from the top. My shoes are a bit soft by now. Each jump on to *pointe* registers more painfully than it did the first time, but I'm too much in awe of the choreographer to ask for time out to change to a new, harder pair. It's short, I'm a quick learner (and Philip's helpful interventions dissolve the mysteries of the score) and so I run through without mistakes. He's pleased and so am I. 'OK, thank you. See you tomorrow.' I retreat to the back of the room where track pants, fleece, shoe bag, handbag and water bottle are shoved against the wall, under the *barre*, to pull on the extra clothes and gather up my belongings before I head off towards the changing room, a bite to eat, and the evening's performance.

Adding to the Repertoire

New work like this is vital to the creative health of any ballet company: it ensures that the art form remains relevant in a contemporary and diverse world, it challenges artists to find new dimensions within themselves and encourages audiences to revisit their preconceptions about what dance can be. However, most ballet companies developed a healthy culture of new work for pragmatic as well as philosophical reasons. In the UK and the US, where ballet really took hold only between the two world wars, there just weren't enough works in the repertoire to populate a season without adding new ones at regular intervals.

Ballets have been staged since the early sixteenth century, but because there was no standardised method of writing them down – unlike music – precious little of this early work survives. The oldest extant ballets still danced in anything like their original form – no more than a handful – are from the mid-nineteenth century, and so the bulk of ballet's repertoire has been built, out of necessity, over the last hundred years. Between George Balanchine in the US and Frederick

Ashton and Kenneth MacMillan in the UK – three of the most significant and prolific ballet choreographers of the twentieth century – an astonishing 650 ballets were created in the years from 1920 to 1992.

At The Royal Ballet, the importance of new work is reinforced all the way through the school and into professional life. Students study choreography as part of the curriculum and have the opportunity each year to create short ballets for annual performances. Serving as bodies for our friends' efforts, as well as creating our own, exposed us for the first time to the challenges of crafting something original from ballet's long-defined language. Most of our efforts were tame and polite, the dance equivalent of cucumber sandwiches with crusts removed, but some dancers, even then, emerged as possessing the courage to stand out.

I remember Mark Sieczkarek casting a very young Michael Clark as 'the outsider', a boy who hid his green face inside a paper bag, in a piece that was considered outrageously bold, not least because it was choreographed to pop music. 'An outstanding piece of work, but I do wish you'd find your inspiration on Radio 3 rather than Radio 1,' was the judges' summation.

In the company, regular choreographic workshops, to which dancers commit their time on a voluntary basis, have been part of the annual programme since 1967 and serve as a laboratory for creative talent, a platform on which young dancers can explore and reveal hidden facets of themselves, a crucible for new ideas and a place to experiment with innovative ways of making dance.

Off Schedule, Off Piste

All choreographers have their own, preferred, ways of working: some are more active than others, some arrive with steps already prepared, some use the dancers' bodies like clay, moulding the choreography around their movement style. Some like to tell stories, some prefer symbolism and metaphor, and some are happiest making movement that has no explicit meaning at all. While some choreographers put together traditional steps in innovative combinations, others stretch and distort the familiar ballet technique to create unfamiliar physical languages – off kilter, off balance and sometimes off the wall. But whatever the approach, throughout ballet's history, there has – by and large – been a hierarchical relationship between the choreographer and the dancers, with the choreographer responsible for generating the ideas and the dancers responsible for taking them on and trying them out.

Over recent years, as the divergent worlds of contemporary dance and ballet have been drawn closer together again, alternative ways of making dance have found their way into the ballet studio. Now, dancers might be asked to play a collaborative role in creating the steps, to work with alternative logic or unrelated external stimuli in an attempt to outwit the natural human tendency to favour pattern and symmetry, which have been the basis of Western art for so very long.

Inspired by the American choreographer Merce Cunningham, dance-makers might surrender the structuring of their works to decisions based on chance. I once worked with a choreographer who made a piece by creating six sequences of movement and then allocating them to six numbered dancers, each choice determined by a throw of the dice.

Other choreographers use images, words or designs as the stimulus for movement, a method we explored with Siobhan Davies, when dancers from her company and The Royal Ballet collaborated on a piece called *13 Different Keys*. She arrived in the studio armed with a pile of books – art, photography, architecture, design, icons, tapestries and more – and asked us each to pick one and turn it into movement. The initial Jack and Jill response, which was simply to trace the shape on the floor, progressed only when, out of desperation, came the notion that perhaps we might use some other body part, rather than just the feet, to create the pattern. Arms, for instance. Once we'd made that (not very) imaginative leap, we moved on to other, less obvious bits of the anatomy – hips, stomach, elbows or ear – before turning the pattern around and creating it vertically, backwards or while lying on the floor.

Perhaps most perplexing, for those of us trained within the norms of classical ballet, is the alternative relationship between movement and music that contemporary dance explores. In ballet, music almost always comes first, providing the direct inspiration for the steps or, at the very least, a bed on which the steps lie. The movement and the music combine to create a third entity, a creation greater than the constituent parts. Some contemporary choreographers reject this dependency of movement on music and create the dance separately before placing the two elements alongside one another, allowing each to co-exist rather than to merge into one. They may even try out several possible pairings of music and dance before settling on a final version.

Cunningham – perhaps the godfather of contemporary dance-making – would frequently create works in which the music, the design and the dance met for the first time on the first night, with the only point in common the fact that they were being performed at the same time. This independence of each element is very much at odds with ballet's tradition, more a modern partnership than a conventional marriage. Or, at least, it's closer to the kind of marriage Khalil Gibran's Prophet recommends: stand together, yet not too near together.

Deconstructive Construction

For most of my career, these contemporary approaches were the exception, something we were able to experiment with off schedule, in the regular choreographic workshops or in extra-curricular projects. It was through one of these projects, towards the end of my dancing life, that I met Wayne McGregor, choreographer and dancer, and now Resident Choreographer with The Royal Ballet, when we were both booked to appear on a tiny stage in a former music hall, in Brick Lane, as part of London's Dance Umbrella festival.

Wayne danced a gyroscopic solo of radial movement, legs and arms blurring into great arcs of light. It was like dance seen at slow shutter-speed, fragmented, mesmerising, beautiful and unprecedented. Every rule seemed to be broken, every given challenged, and yet there was an indisputable logic at the heart of what he did. At the time, Wayne's work was almost entirely in contemporary dance, but it was immediately obvious that connecting his extraordinary curiosity, intelligence and vision with the extraordinary potential of the classically trained body was more than just important; it was essential. And so Wayne agreed to work with a self-selecting group of dancers, in our free time, just to see where it would take us.

These were rehearsals like none I had ever known. Instead of establishing the usual hierarchy in the studio, by settling on the chairs at the front, Wayne seemed determined to occupy the same space as the dancers. There was no void between us: we were in it together. The beginning of the rehearsal came with almost no warning, a smooth segue from the social interaction preceding it. Unleashing a sequence of unrecognisable movements at whirlwind speed and creating his own onomatopoeic rhythmic pulse, he barely stopped for breath before suggesting, 'Let's have a little try.' We fumbled through, tripping up over angles and accents never previously encountered. Not only were the movements new, the sequencing of them bore no relation to our familiar movement vocabulary.

A generalisation, but in ballet, for the most part, certain small movements precede bigger ones, and linking steps are just that. It's like a language, with verbs and nouns working harder than conjunctions, for instance. Here, there was no such convention. And just as it's harder to retain a random series of words in which there is no narrative arc, it's harder to remember a collection of steps that don't appear, within the context of your existing dance experience, to have an overarching structure.

Learning new sequences always takes time, even when they're made up of the usual steps, and in this new world order we desperately tried to create a fast track by labelling the movements with a word that seemed, however tenuously, to have a connection: *spoon*, *dip*, *slice*. By reciting these labels as we did the steps it was possible to develop a narrative thread, however absurd, offering a chance that we might lock each sequence into our reeling brains.

Successfully landing these initial sequences was not

enough. Before we'd really absorbed them, he was off again creating more, slicing them into segments and reconstructing in random order. Next, he asked us to take the arms from one sequence and the legs from another and combine them into a new phrase. Then the maths came in: this group try the first, third and seventh movements; this group try the second and fifth and then the first; this group does the second, pauses for three, then the fifth and six . . . Next it was directions: 'Do the first section facing the back, then turn 90 degrees for each subsequent movement.' Without pausing to allow us to assimilate these foreign instructions he set us off again: 'Just have a little go.'

All the familiar dimensions were interrogated: speed, order, direction, plane. We felt like novice dancers again, unable to follow instructions at this kind of speed and incapable of repeating a movement with any degree of precision. And then, when our brains were as scrambled as the choreography, we moved into another dimension altogether: 'Pick a point in the room and describe it with your hips.' Eh? They didn't teach us that at White Lodge.

Three whistlestop hours later, we had created a palette of movement that would define the piece and that could be taken in any order, any combination and any time frame. He wrapped up as quickly as he had started. The tornado had passed and each of us went away to start the process of making sense of it.

Over the next few weeks, some of those initial ideas were transformed yet again into duets or trios, made to travel, shifted in time and space or put into canon. Wayne functioned like an editor, choosing the bits he wanted to retain and deciding how they would be put together. At some point, having worked with various alternatives, he settled on a selection of music and merged it with the movement, establishing the two as equal partners on a single stage. The piece, when it was shown, was aptly titled *Symbionts*.

And the dancers, like the music, were partners in this collaborative process. We had shifted from a more familiar role as re-creative artist (re-creating given steps) to creative artist (an active contributor to a new choreographic language). This was both liberating and terrifying at the same time. A familiar anxiety dream for dancers is a variation of the more normal exam scenario: you're standing on the middle of the stage, with the music about to begin, but you have absolutely no idea what you're supposed to be dancing. These early attempts at sharing in the creative process felt a bit like one of those dreams made real.

Every time dancers encounter these new approaches, these rule-breakers, we have to let go of something we've been trained to hold dear – narrative thread, dance mirroring music, square hips, or blithe ease –

and we grow in the process. Each transgression is a reminder that it's only through artists who dare to be different that the art form moves forwards. So much of ballet's culture, necessarily, encourages conformity – the very concept of a *corps de ballet* depends on it – yet to create something new, choreographers have to be prepared to step out of line.

If the idea is genuinely original, there is (and should be) a chance that it won't quite come off. Choreographers take huge risks, laying themselves bare first through the creative process and then again on the first night, when the world – always hungry for the next big thing – comes along to pronounce judgement. Whenever I entered a rehearsal studio to work on something new, I imagined that the choreographer had all the answers and that the nerves were entirely on our side. Only now, looking back, do I realise that the choreographer at the front might well have been just as nervous as the dancers, huddling together towards the back.

6.55 The Half-hour Call

'Good evening, ladies and gentlemen: that was the half-hour call. Would all guests of artists and staff now leave the Opera House via the stage door.'

6.55-and-a-bit, and the stage-door announcement follows immediately on from the stage manager's half-hour call. Everyone out. The sentence construction implies a question but there was no rising intonation in the delivery and anyway, for me, it was never a question I needed consider. The suggestion that at that point, so close to the show, I might have space – in either my head or my dressing-room – to entertain a guest always struck me as totally bizarre.

The half-hour call is a brief moment of calm between storms, a hiatus in the rollercoaster of harnessed energy that leads up to performance and which is performance itself. With thirty-five minutes to go before curtain-up, time is still – just – on your side. You could, if needs be, change shoes, make-up, costume, your partner, or even your role. All these things can, and do, happen. Dancers have even been known to change their minds and head home, but even in that extreme scenario, the show would still go on. Half an hour is enough time to deal with most emergencies.

Head down to the wings at 6.55 and all is quiet. You will probably see the stage managers relaxed and chatting, a privileged visitor enjoying a quick tour of the set (notwithstanding the stage-door announcement) and a lone dancer trying out steps on the stage. But don't be fooled: this ordered calm belies the frenzy of activity that has gone before and that is about to ensue.

Go back half an hour in time, and the scene is a different one altogether. The Royal Opera House presents both The Royal Opera and The Royal Ballet on its main stage, with five or six productions in performance at any one time (more, if the ballet is presenting a mixed programme of one-act works). There are three sessions on the stage each day and the crew works a sixteen-hour shift: a morning rehearsal (either for the technical teams alone, or with the companies), an evening show, and the afternoon changeover. On a double-show day, with the matinee starting at perhaps 1 o'clock, the changeover has to be managed in double-quick time, particularly if the two performances are of different repertoire.

The morning rehearsal generally finishes around 3 o'clock and, over the next four hours, a miracle of transformation takes place as the technicians effect the change into the evening show: forests become palaces, ruins become taverns, market squares become salons. The crew, in true Henry Higgins style, treats each with the same careful respect and easy pragmatism in equal measures, the duchess's boudoir equal to the flowergirl's stall. Each individual seems to understand exactly his contribution to the whole and makes it without any apparent instruction. It's like watching ants at work.

First, the props have to be cleared and the scenery packed tightly together on the centre of the stage, each piece in its allotted place, like a three-dimensional jigsaw. Then, with a warning call of 'wagons moving', the floor starts to shift and the entire set glides off stage, on a rolling wagon. It's like watching a landslide. The stage is now clear: it resembles nothing so much as an empty aircraft hangar.

Then the process starts again, in reverse. Bars are lowered from high up in the fly tower and new scenery cloths and lights attached before they are flown back up out of sight. A new set, pre-built in the side-stage areas on a specially sprung 'ballet wagon', glides into place on the moving floors and the final, smaller pieces are carried in by hand to be positioned exactly on pre-ordained marks.

Stage electrics starts the business of focusing the lights while props are laid out, either on the set or on the prop table in the wings, where the dancers will find them ready for use. The resin tray is put in place, a giant roll of tissue paper – to cover any emergency – close to hand. By 6.55, the stage is set, the lighting finished and the crew is on its break. The stage enjoys a rare moment of tranquillity, that state of total stillness which can be achieved only between heartbeats.

In the *corps de ballet* dressing-rooms downstairs, it's not quite so relaxed. The half-hour is, contractually, the latest time a dancer can arrive for a show, and the time at which covers must be in the building to check that the cast is fit and healthy and they aren't required to step in. In truth, it's rare for anyone to cut it this fine, but it's fair to say that the *corps de ballet* dancers are unlikely to have commenced preparations for the show as early as the principals and, by the half, they might have some catching up to do. For a start, their studio rehearsals have probably not finished until 5.30 and the next half-hour will have been spent taking a shower and getting something to eat.

But the *corps* is on every night and there is less riding on their individual shoulders than on the shoulders of tonight's leads. With the absence of pressure and the familiarity of routine, it's perfectly possible to manage make-up, wig, shoes and costumes in well under an hour. Digesting takes a little longer.

The Dressing-Room . . .

My first experience of the *corps de ballet* dressing-room was the Ballet Room, a long room to the rear of the stage and down one flight of cold stone stairs. Ancient lino covered its floor and a long, fixed table ran down its middle, a silvered, double-sided mirror rising from its central spine and perhaps ten or twelve places on either side. The 'places' were denoted by upright chairs and bare, bright light bulbs screwed into the mirror, end on to the artist, in the usual theatre style. Under the surface of the table were pairs of lockers, each with three dusty shelves: the locker on one side of each pair was for the ballet company, the locker on the other side for the opera. Each night, before the show, we had to get out our make-up and set up our place and then, before we left the building, put it all away again. This had gone on for years until the first phase of the redevelopment of the Royal Opera House, in 1982, created new changing rooms for the opera company, leaving the Ballet Room for the ballet company alone.

Washing facilities in the Ballet Room were rudimentary. A row of low basins along one wall served as a place for washing faces, laundering tights and for applying water-based coloured pancake to shoes and ribbons, when the role required it, leaving the edges of the basins permanently stained with a rainbow of differing hues. When first I used the room, there were no showers available for the *corps*. Later, a small room alongside was converted into a massive walk-in shower. Far less stylish than it sounds, it was, simply, a room. The lino on the floor had been replaced with tiles, drains inserted and six showerheads installed around the edge, but it was still just a room. The ladies of the *corps de ballet* showered here together, ankle deep in each other's grubby water.

The dressing-room contained the dust and the

debris of decades. Shelves and hooks had been added wherever there was space. Dressing-gowns hung on doors and over chairbacks, headdress and wig boxes were crammed in, stacked high. Pink shoes with tangled ribbons nestled under every chair and dangled above every place. Wicker baskets and costume rails lined the walls. The net of upturned tutus scratched at bare arms as you brushed past. The smell was of face powder, wig glue, hairspray and the shellac we used endlessly to reinforce our shoes. With dusty windows to one side overlooking a brick wall and the bare bulbs burning from early morning until late in the evening, our days and nights merged into one.

It was, above all, a rather public place. There were no corners to hide in, no chance to slip away when it all got too much, and nowhere to stretch out between shows. Those naked light bulbs shone their harsh glare on friendships, fallings-out and love affairs. No conversation could be private, no correction discreet. Those *corps de ballet* dancers who leapfrogged the system and danced solo roles did so from their place in this basement and returned there afterwards. Generally, the atmosphere was supportive and congratulatory. On rare occasions, it could be uncomfortably silent.

To one side of this room was a second, smaller, room where more senior *corps de ballet* dancers went; a sort of dressing-room purgatory from which a few dancers emerged on promotion to soloist. Some dancers made it into the room but never left. Others, after perhaps five or six years downstairs, were promoted to soloist and moved one floor up, into a row of five rooms, each with space for three or four dancers: the Ladies' Principal Dressing-Rooms.

These rooms directly behind the stage – Dressing-Rooms 1–5 – no longer exist, but perhaps they should have been preserved: re-created, at least, for the sake of the history of which they were such a part. British ballet was created by artists for whom these rooms were home: Margot Fonteyn, Beryl Grey, Moira Shearer, Antoinette Sibley, Lynn Seymour, Monica Mason, Darcey Bussell and more. On the floor directly above, an identical set of rooms housed the men: over the years, dancers such as Robert Helpmann, Michael Somes, Rudolf Nureyev, Anthony Dowell, David Wall, Jonathan Cope. These dancers returned to those rooms having made history in brand new ballets by Frederick Ashton and Kenneth MacMillan, ballets that went on to become modern classics and the cornerstones of twentieth-century repertoire around the world.

But then the rooms weren't much to write home about – if you discount the 'I've been promoted!' letter, which was always worth the cost of a stamp. Their style owed much to the Ballet Room below. The same carpenter must have fashioned the work benches and lockers, and the same electrician mounted the bulbs on the mirrors. The window frames and doors were thick with paint: right angles had morphed into curves long ago as layer was applied on glossy layer, giving the woodwork an air of Gaudí. In each room, there was a single sink, a floor-length mirror and, by my time, a brown, velour, Parker Knoll reclining chair. On the floor by the door we had our own resin tray and, alongside it, a big plastic container of shellac, thick, gloopy stains marking its spot. The room was perhaps 12 feet by 6 feet, and it was home to four of us.

Those rooms were our refuge, at least during performances and stage calls, for most of our performing life. It's not surprising that the dressing-rooms in the newly developed Royal Opera House, post-1999, were of prime importance to the dancers, who began thinking about the design in the early 1980s, an astonishing two decades before the building work took place.

My diary entry for 19 April 1982 records a company meeting to discuss the 'new development' and the same year a group of us attended a meeting at principal dancer David Drew's flat where the single agenda item was the detailed design of the ideal dressing-room. As the funding for the redevelopment would not be in place until at least 1995, this was forward thinking on an impressive scale.

By the time those rooms came to be built, they were to the dancers' exact stipulations, right down to special shelves where shellac could be added to shoes and slatted racks where they could then be left to dry out, thus avoiding any glutinous mess on the floor. Within weeks of moving into our purpose-designed quarters, the shellac shelf was the same patchwork of thick, treacle-coloured lumps that had characterised the floor in Rooms 1–5.

Preparing to Dance the Lead

For the evening's principals, preparation for the show starts much earlier in the day than it does for the dancers of the *corps*. If it's a tough show, the scheduler will usually try to give the principals the afternoon off, which means you can head home, try for a nap and eat lunch in your own kitchen before setting out for the theatre. The content of this pre-performance meal is all-important – plenty of carbohydrates and not much fat – and the timing crucial. With food taking around four hours to pass into the small intestine – which is where you want it – and the show starting at 7.30, lunch at 3 o'clock is ideal. (I usually went for pasta with tomato sauce.) Time it right and the carbohydrates will release their energy to fuel the performance. Leave it too late and you'll still be feeling bloated and full when the curtain goes up.

The stage door, around 5 o'clock, is at its quietest. Inside, in offices above and around the stage, the theatre's admin staff will be at their desks for another hour yet and most of the people involved with the show have still to arrive. The technical crew is hard at work on stage, effecting the change between afternoon rehearsal and evening perform- ance. There's no sign yet of any bouquets, which may or may not arrive for the principals and soloists. But the stage-door staff will greet the incoming princi- pals with a knowing look: it's an unofficial element of their job, to know what's on that evening and who is dancing.

If it's a debut, there may be cards waiting and they'll be handed over with cheery good wishes. They might, on occasion, request a signature on a photograph or a programme left by a fan, but many dancers will refuse to oblige at this point, promising to deal with it later. Never sign anything before a performance: it was Anthony Dowell's superstition. As I never saw him give a bad performance I figured it was one worth acquiring for myself.

Upstairs, if you're lucky, the room is yours alone. The hours before a show are private time and other people in the room can interrupt the routine on which you lean for support. If it's a familiar role, the interrup- tions matter less, but if you feel exposed and unsure it's helpful to have the space to yourself. I only once made the mistake of inviting guests – no, worse than guests – to share the hours leading up to the show.

One of the earlier TV reality shows – *Paddington Green* – was gearing up and as an almost local res- ident, I had been lined up to participate. It was all going well, from my perspective, and I'd been filmed on several occasions: at home, out at the local shops, in rehearsal and now the crew wanted to film me getting ready for *Swan Lake*.

As I put on make-up and prepared my shoes, the producer fired questions at me from her seat out of shot: how does it feel to be nearing the end of your career? Are you constantly aware of the youngsters coming up behind you? Do you ever wonder whether you're still up to it? The angle they planned to take with my story slowly dawned on me as, question by question, she chipped away at my self-esteem.

I politely asked if I might be left alone. Could we perhaps do this some other time? Perhaps we could set up the situation, when I wasn't actually performing? I clearly hadn't got the point of reality TV, and the producing team didn't call again.

5.10 – Hair and Make-up

With the room to yourself, you set up camp in your allotted place. Cards are opened, read and stuck around the mirror's frame. A selection of shoes – each a contender for the show – is pulled from a bag and lined up on an empty place alongside, coddled together in pairs, one shoe nestling inside the other and the ribbons tucked away inside. Street clothes are exchanged for soft ballet shoes and warm socks, a comfortable leotard, woollen leggings or tracksuit pants, with a zip-front fleece on top. (The front fastening is important: once your make-up is finished, and the wig or headdress in place, nothing goes over your head.) Hair, for now, is pinned loosely out of the way – the wig mistress will deal with it later – and various pots and jars come out of a large, flat-bottomed sponge bag: foundation, powder, eye-shadow, mascara, blusher, lipstick as well as a selection of brushes, sponges and powder puffs. Sitting in front of the lit mirror, in eerie calm, it's time to put on the make-up.

Over the thirty years in which I was dancing, stage make-up became more and more streamlined, at least in comparison to the war paint they taught us to apply at school. The kit list, when we joined The Royal Ballet Upper School, went something like this: fishing-tackle box (honestly); Leichner foundation sticks (two colours, an ivory and an orange, which were each applied in thick stripes and then blended together to form a creamy beige mask); a brick-red stick that was added to the cheeks and under the eyebrows; brown and crimson-lake sticks, for eyes and lips respectively; false eyelashes and glue; and heavy powder, to fix it all together. Oh, and a pot of greasy Cremine (think goose fat) to get it all off.

We had make-up classes once a week and struggled to make ourselves look anything other than absurd in the traditional stage make-up that had been handed down from generation to generation: thick, imperme-able base, heavy black 'tram lines' above and below the eyes with red dots at the inside and outside corners. Solid arched eyebrows and rosebud lips completed the look. How did the ballerinas of yesteryear make it look so stylish, elegant and appropriate? I looked like a man in drag.

Most of us persevered with the 'proper' approach for our first few months in the company. Alessandra Ferri, who sat alongside me and at whose healthy disregard for tradition-for-its-own-sake I could only marvel, soon moved away from the *Princess Tina* approach and adopted a style of make-up inspired by the pages of *Vogue*, all softly blended shading and natural tones. The older company members had abandoned the dots and tram lines long ago. It made sense of course: both theatre lighting and long-distance spectacles have improved enormously over the last fifty years. Generally, audiences can see much more clearly – there's no longer the need for a dancer's facial features to shout.

There is something satisfyingly ritualistic about the application of make-up, an age-old symbol of the preparation for an occasion of import. I thought back to my many hours spent applying make-up when I saw those pictures of one of the remaining uncontacted tribes in the Amazon. In the first picture, you see some fifty or so people scattering on hearing the plane high above their thatched settlement. In the second picture, taken minutes later, the tribe has reappeared, armed with arrows and with red and black paint applied to their bodies, ready now to face this unfamiliar threat.

Similarly, in Kenneth MacMillan's *Rite of Spring*, the elders add black stripes to the Chosen Maiden's face before she embarks on her last, sacrificial, dance. The first dots of foundation on my forehead, cheeks and chin have something of this feel about them: a first preparation and protection for an encounter with the unknown.

The whole making-up process, from foundation to the final lipstick, lasts half an hour, at the most. Make-up for the camera takes much longer, particularly with the cruel, all-seeing lenses of High Definition. But for the stage, it can all be much less perfect and I always bore in mind the advice of Michael Coleman, witty and wonderful principal dancer of The Royal Ballet in the 1970s: 'All anyone sees is two black holes where the eyes should be and a red blob for the mouth.' Not quite true, but his healthy scepticism over how much time is usefully spent on precision was worth remembering. Aim for definition and then add lots of powder, pressed into the skin rather than wiped across: that way, it holds the make-up in place, however sweaty you get.

With make-up complete, you wait for the wig mistress to come and do your hair or, depending on the ballet, to put on your wig. She arrives at about 6 o'clock, armed with a large box of pins, grips, glue and scissors and gets to work. If a wig is required for the role, you might already have prepared the ground by 'pin-curling' your hair under a stocking-top, each separate pin-curl secured with two grips, in the shape of a cross. The pin-curls provide anchor points to which the wig can be secured and once your head is covered in these unsightly dots and bumps, a cut-off stocking-top is added on top, like a beanie hat, fixed in place with small pins at both temples and centre back.

Ballet wigs are made of human hair, attached to a material base, with sheer netting around the hairline at the front and down past the temples (where a man's sideburns would be). The wig arrives ready dressed: gloriously piled curls, intricately braided plaits, long and luscious locks, depending on the role. It may have taken up to an hour to prepare and so the wig mistress leaves it safely in the box until the last possible moment. She checks the pin-curls for security and tidies away any individual straggling hairs, pushing them under the stocking-top with the tail of her comb.

Satisfied that the foundations are secure, she removes the dressed wig from its box, pulls out the ball of scrunched tissue paper that has been keeping it in shape and stands by to put it on your head. Automatically, without prompting, you present two index fingers at your temples, like little goat's horns, hooking the net at the front in position while the wig mistress pulls the back down at the nape of your neck. Once the wig is comfortably in place, she opens a pot of thick, honey-coloured glue and, forcing the net away from your face with the tail comb, paints a generous blob at the top of the cheek bones, alongside your ears, and at the centre of the forehead, close to the hairline. With a dampened make-up sponge, she presses the net against your glued face until it is well and truly stuck. Once the front of the wig is secure, hairpins are added, strategically positioned in among the curls, to fix the whole thing tightly to the pin-curls beneath your stocking-top. A blast of hairspray finishes it off.

However demanding the choreography, however rough the partnering, no curl must escape and the wig must not move. Ideally, you should be able to forget you're wearing it. Anyone who has seen some of the wigs ballet dancers have to wear – for instance, in the big costume ballets like *Manon*, or *Mayerling* – will appreciate the challenge this presents. The wig I wore in *Manon* was a glamorous heap of golden curls – it was the hairstyle Mrs Thatcher dreamed of – and it stood at least six inches proud of my head on all sides. It weighed, I'm sure, several pounds.

Generally, you get the services of the wig masters and mistresses only if you're dancing the principal and soloist roles. The dancers of the *corps de ballet*, by and large, have to fend for themselves and it doesn't always go too well. I remember one dancer gradually losing her wig during the townspeople's port-side dance, at the beginning of the third act of *Manon*. It started to slide early on and, as the dance progressed, more and more of the unsightly stocking-top beneath was revealed. We were all horribly transfixed, willing it to stay put for just a few more bars, but as the dance came to its climax the wig dropped neatly to the floor and lay there, accusingly, at the dancer's feet.

The dancer, always a supremely stylish artist, retained her dignity, despite the fact that her eighteenth-century costume was now topped off with what looked like a bank robber's headgear: when the music and the dance had finished, she simply swooped to the floor, picked it up and placed it under her arm, stroking it gently and cooing just a little, as if her adored lap dog had misbehaved.

For some roles there is no wig, just a headdress worn atop your own hair. Sometimes, there are no embellishments at all. Even so, for principal roles, the wig mistress will still come along to do your hair. Her confident calm is part of the pre-performance ritual: it takes away some of the pressure and some of the responsibility, too. If the *fouettés* fail, you have only yourself to blame. If your hair were to come down . . . well, it wouldn't be your fault. For me, the best thing about having my hair done was that moment of peace it provided, perhaps even a sense of comfort and security, the feeling a little girl enjoys as her mother plaits her hair ready for school. There, there, it's all going to be fine.

6.15 – Warming up

By now, it's around 6.15 and there's an hour and a quarter before the curtain goes up. With wig fixed or hair gelled and sprayed, you pick up your bottle, pull on track pants or leg warmers, stuff the leading contenders for this evening's footwear into a bag and head up to the studio to warm up. Prior to the redevelopment of the Royal Opera House, warm-up for the show took place in a corner of the wings, a piece of scenery a makeshift *barre*. Now, the dancers have the luxury of studio space just a few floors above the stage.

The pre-show warm-up is not just a repeat of the morning's class, although to the untrained eye it may look similar. For a start, it's likely to be a private affair: there may be a handful of dancers using the same studio, but each will inhabit their own space and construct their own warm-up, based on their individual needs. Some companies provide a formal pre-show warm-up, led by a teacher and with a pianist to accompany but, in general, class is provided in the morning only, with pre-show warming up the responsibility of the individual.

Without a teacher to set the exercises or determine the pace, the dancer is free to focus on those parts of the body which require specific attention: a troublesome joint, a stiff muscle, a tight hamstring. This might mean starting out on the floor, perhaps borrowing elements from Pilates or yoga, before moving through a précis of a regular class *barre*, with only the briefest of pauses to change sides or work out an exercise that 'scans'. A few straightforward jumps in the basic positions – on two feet, not one – and gentle stretches of hamstrings, calves and the back round it all up. A few steps from the performance ahead might be incorporated into the process.

Without the interruptions necessary in a formal class environment – for teaching the exercises or making corrections – a dancer can warm up effectively in around fifteen to twenty minutes. The sensible dancer will stick to familiar and safe routines: the hour before performance is not the time to attempt new or difficult *enchaînements*. Getting warm, rather than mastering challenges, is the aim at this point. Everest can be tackled afresh tomorrow morning.

6.35 – *The Shoe Ceremony*

Fully warm, with hair and make-up complete, it's time to face the *pointe* shoes. While much of this pre-show ritual is common both to male and female dancers, the agony of the *pointe* shoe is unique to the women – with, inevitably, the odd exception; Bottom in Frederick Ashton's *The Dream*, for instance, requires the male dancer playing the role to dance on *pointe*. Let me be clear: the agony is not physical. From time to time, toes 'skin' and blisters form (and soft corns are a hazard of the job) but the human body will take almost anything you throw at it, as long as you throw it systematically and over time. So *pointe* work, with proper training, is not, in itself, painful, at least not for a professional dancer. No, the agony is emotional.

The *pointe* shoe wields an undue degree of power over its wearer. Each brand-new pair, so pink and shiny, holds the possibility that here, at last, are the perfect shoes: light as air, flexible as kid leather yet supportive as a girdle . . . effortlessly moulding to your feet and lasting for ever. And each time, the awful reality reveals itself: like lovers, no shoe is ever quite perfect. And so, like unsuitable lovers, the shoes play too great a role in our emotional well-being, our self-confidence and our state of inner harmony, all of them hostage to the innocent pink shoes. A bad shoe – or a shoe perceived to be bad – can ruin a performance and yet, strangely, it might be exactly the shoe that dances like a dream the following week. So perhaps it's not just the shoes: clearly, there are complex factors at play here.

Each dancer has her favoured method of preparing shoes and the ones she tests immediately before a show will already have been the subject of a rigorous audition process. Mine involved a preliminary once-over for each pair, testing them for strength, flexibility, shape and feel, before 'shellac-ing' them with a thin coating of clear wood knotting poured into the tip of the toe and worked around the block in the way a taster swills wine around a glass. The next day, once the shellac was dry, I'd take a sturdy pair of scissors and remove the Thumbelina-sized nail that fixes the insole to the outer sole, underneath the heel. The nail's head is buried in the insole and to get it out you have to slide the blade of a pair of scissors under the insole, loosening the glue holding it down and gradually worrying the nail free. Once it was removed, I'd gently bend the last two inches of both the inner and outer sole, taking care not to snap them completely, trying to introduce flexibility without destroying support. Then I'd slip the shoe on and try it out.

Was the inside smooth and free from ridges? Did it naturally guide my foot into the ideal position or did it hold me back, forcing me to fight against the shoe in order to get my body weight forwards? If that was the case I knew *pirouettes* would be impossible and the muscles under my feet would cramp from the constant effort of trying to find a state of balance. More dangerous were the shoes that forced the instep in the other direction: they looked ravishing, creating erotic curves out of the instep, but this enforced arch was likely to endanger the Achilles tendon and the delicate tissues at the rear of the ankle joint. The shoes that held my foot back might be retained for a second opinion, on a different day. The ones that forced it forwards were rejected, mercilessly, without a second thought.

The shoes surviving this first audition were next beaten against a concrete floor or a metal stage weight – six or eight firm bashes to each shoe, to soften them up a little and reduce the noise. I'd then take a Stanley knife and slice off the satin at the tip of the shoe – the part you stand on when dancing on *pointe*. I'd given up darning at White Lodge and wasn't sorry to be shot of the endless hours it consumed, or the pinhole pricks in my fingertips that never seemed to heal. Besides, the hessian layer beneath the satin gives a far better grip on the floor. Turning the shoes over, I'd score the underside of each sole, gouging out diagonal lines one way then the other, to help prevent slipping.

Next came the ribbons, each one cut to length, the ends singed (to prevent fraying) and then sewn to the shoe's canvas inner layer, sloping slightly towards the front of the foot and taking care not to stitch right through to the satin itself. I can't begin to calculate how many pairs of ribbons I attached to shoes over the course of my dancing career . . . two ribbons per shoe, two shoes per pair, perhaps five pairs per week, for twenty years as a professional and seven as a student. Not surprising, then, that I had it down to a fine art: at my fastest, I could complete the task in well under five minutes.

With ribbons attached, I'd wear each pair for ten or fifteen minutes – no more – in class or a low-pressure rehearsal, before taking them off, adding more shellac and leaving them to dry. Only at this point could I tell which pairs might actually be eligible for a performance.

Each dancer favours different types of shoes on stage. Some cannot bear new shoes and continue wearing older, softer pairs until they fall off their feet. (Sometimes, events dictate this: on tour in Cuba, Leanne Benjamin found herself with only one old pair of shoes when her luggage failed to arrive. She danced several performances of Frederick Ashton's *Thaïs pas de deux* and one *Giselle* before conceding that she really didn't think she could squeeze another show out of them. Luckily her luggage arrived that day.) Other dancers favour harder shoes, wearing brand new at every performance.

Most of us choose shoes depending on the demands of the role. For *Swan Lake*, you might consider three pairs, one for each act. The pair selected for the second, 'white', act need staying power: the *pas de deux* proper is close to ten minutes long and the left shoe in particular bears the brunt of the slow, sustained choreography. The third, 'black', act (although its technical demands are more obvious) is in fact more straightforward but the pressures on that left foot – in particular the thirty-two *fouettés* – mean you select your shoes with special care. The shoes for the final act may never make it on to your feet. By that point, you're often too exhausted (and, if it's gone well, relieved) to make the change.

With about forty minutes to go before curtain-up, it's time to make the final decision between the seven or eight possibilities lined up on the floor. My finalists had descriptive jottings on their soles, from the pre-selection process: 'good'; 'bit back'; 'possible Act 3'; or just a confused '?'. Each pair is slipped on, ribbons loosely tied, and a few sample steps executed. A test *pirouette* is essential, a *relevé* or two a good idea, but you know when a shoe feels right. A good shoe is, most definitely, like the best kind of partner: strong and supportive, but so comfortable that you could almost forget it's there.

The shoes that don't make the grade tonight are put to one side. On another occasion, with a different role, different choreography or a different mood, they might be just what's needed. Armed with the chosen pairs, it's time to head back to the dressing-room. They're about to call the half.

6.55 – The Half-hour Call

Almost two hours after tonight's principals arrived in the theatre, the stage manager calls the half-hour: 'Good evening, ladies and gentlemen, this is the half-hour call for tonight's performance of *Sleeping Beauty*. Half an hour please.' It's the first time, of many, that her unruffled tones will be heard across the evening.

It's the cue to shift up a gear. Your hair is finished but there's a headdress still to add and your make-up is likely to need a touch-up: fresh lipstick, as well as a final dab of powder above the top lip and across your brow. The shoes have been selected now but they're lying to one side: first, there are plasters to apply.

The plaster routine is every bit as personal as the shoe ceremony, involving custom-shaped fragments of plaster (or melolin and micropore – kinder to the skin), corn felt, shock-absorbent rubber pads and a space-age blancmange-like substance we called squidge. This painstaking process is an insurance policy against the discomfort of bleeding toes, worth every second of the extra time it takes.

With toes safe from harm, you pull on pink tights, taking care not to dislodge the dressings. Finally, a little spit in the heel of each shoe and a scratch in the sticky resin tray ensure that the shoes stay attached to your feet. Ribbons are tied firmly, but not tightly, double knots tucked neatly on the inside of the ankle and perhaps stitched into place, just to be sure.

By now, it's coming up to the quarter: 7.10, and time to get dressed. It can take anything from thirty seconds to ten minutes to get into costume: generally, the more recent the ballet, the smaller the costume, although this isn't always the case. Tutus may look complicated but they are relatively straightforward to wear. You step into a tutu as you step into a swimming costume, one foot after the other through the two leg holes, then arms through the straps. The stiff, petersham waistband is fastened first, centre back, an industrial-size hook and eye ensuring it won't come undone. Then a row of smaller hooks and eyes stretching down the basque, snug around the hips, from which layers of tulle extend outwards in all directions by up to half a metre.

It's like wearing a vast, net dinner plate, but it feels completely natural. Most of us have grown up in tutus: our proprioceptors seem to have adapted, like a cat's whiskers, to include the additional girth. The bodice is fastened with a second series of hooks and eyes, working upwards: tight at the waist but easing around the ribs to allow room for the dancer to breathe deep when the going gets tough.

Perhaps the most complex costumes are those for the character roles – *Sleeping Beauty's* Queen, for instance – who don't have as much dancing to do: bustles, petticoats, corsets, floor-length dresses, jewels, heels, cloaks and crowns. Ballets such as *Manon* or *Mayerling*, however – relatively recent works, but in period costumes – come close, with boned bodices that have to be laced, frilly knickers, layered petticoats, cloaks, coats, veils, gloves, muffs and hats.

Getting into these costumes takes the longest, but getting used to them takes longer still. You learn early on that there is no point rehearsing in skimpy Lycra if the costume for the role is made up of multiple layers of lace, satin and brocade. When I danced the Mistress in *Manon* I would often warm up in my costume in the hope that as the exercises made my muscles gradually warmer and more pliable, they might work the same magic on the costume.

The easiest, and quickest, costumes to get into are

the leotards and all-overs of ballets by George Balanchine, William Forsythe or Wayne McGregor.
These seem to have got smaller and smaller over the
years, with tights eventually discarded in favour of
bare legs, and pants and vests, like junior-school gym
kit, becoming pretty much the norm.

In all but the last scenario, you'll need the dresser's
help to get into the costume and you can use these
few minutes of stationary calm as a last opportunity to
focus on the challenges ahead. While laces are tight-
ened, poppers popped or eyes hooked, the dancer can
stop for a moment and visualise some of the trickier
moments, think through particular corrections, imagine it all going exactly according to plan.

At 7.20, the stage manager gives the five-minute
call. Bottle in hand, and with track pants or leg warmers added for warmth, you head for the stage. Some
dancers prefer to be ready and on stage earlier than
this, with time to try their solos before the rest of the
cast arrives, while others avoid last-minute practice. I
always worried that if my steps went badly moments
before curtain-up I'd be unsettled. If they went well,
I'd have wasted my quota of good luck for the evening
on a triumph witnessed only by the stage manager
and a few of the technical crew.

Coming into the wings, the brief calm of the half
has given way to a tight, nervous energy, like a thousand gyroscopes in one small space. The stage is filled
with dancers, technicians, ballet staff and the stage-

management team. Dancers jog furiously, throw legs high above their heads, stretch out on the ground and ease recalcitrant muscles. Picking their way through these living obstacles, soloists and principals go through their steps one more time, focusing on the bits that are most troublesome, trying them over and over again. One dancer spins down the diagonal, narrowly missing another who is leaping in the other direction.

A pit full of players, tuning up or picking out their individual challenges from the score, creates a restless soundtrack to the activity on stage. The conductor is deep in discussion with the leading lady about the tempo of her coda. Props are placed in position: wine goblets on a table, scrolls on standby in the wings alongside velvet cushions laden with gifts. A light is refocused.

The stage manager steps out from her place in the prompt corner and calls, 'Beginners, please.' It's twenty-five minutes past seven. Shoe ribbons are untied and retied, more securely this time. A young soloist asks stage management to put out a call for wigs: her hair doesn't feel quite safe. A lump is spotted under the lino: a hammer is produced and the lump is no more. The company director, the *répétiteurs* and the teachers drift off to take their seats in the auditorium, wishing luck as they go. Another night, another show: they watch them all. The assistant stage manager collects the conductor to take him down to the pit: 'Conductor going down.' The oboe's tuning A sounds out and the other players fall into line until a single massed note swells sweetly over the pit. Tonight, there's an overture, allowing the dancers a few more minutes on stage.

The conductor enters the pit and the audience acknowledges his arrival with a polite burst of applause. He shakes the leader's hand, settles his score and raises his baton. It's a freeze-frame moment, infused with the possibility of the greatest evening the theatre will ever see. Out front, the performance has begun: on the other side of the curtain, we're not quite there yet, with dancers still collecting their props and finding their places, noses being blown and ribbons adjusted just one more time. The overture plays on, laying out for the audience the ballet's central theme, the forces of good triumphant over evil.

As the cue approaches, the stage manager issues a warning call: 'Stand by on stage, please. Tabs going out.' There is a subtle shift as the dancers, now poised and in place, assume character: arms mid-gesture, heads and eyes suddenly alert, they are a living *tableau* that will activate the minute the curtains part. 'Go tabs.' A fleeting metallic jingle – like coins jiggled in a pocket – as heavy-duty steel wires take up the tension through a hundred metal rings and then the whoosh of an implosion as up they go. The auditorium is flooded with light from the stage. The curtain is up.

7.30 Curtain Up

The weightless sweep of the thick velvet curtains, as they draw up into the proscenium arch, is the sound of the dancer's deadline, and there is no deadline in the world deadlier than this one. Now, in front of perhaps two thousand people, the dancer draws simultaneously on years of classes and months of rehearsals to create and deliver the perfect performance. At this point, no revisions or amends are possible. No going back, just once more, to make a point more precisely, or to add poetry to the prose. No tweaking the punch line, yet again, before finally pressing send. The moment is now and, what's more, it might be the only one you ever get.

On stage, the tabs now open, the performance is under way and the dancers of the *corps de ballet* are already earning their keep, setting the scene and, through posture, gesture and the manner in which they interact, revealing more about the ballet's style, mood and period than any programme note could ever explain. The orchestra plays on but the principals and soloists are still in the wings, awaiting their cue: depending on the ballet, it can be five or ten minutes, or even an entire act, before they make their first entrance. Still, the curtain is up, the show launched on its way. It would take a power cut, a fire alarm, or worse, to interrupt its inexorable progress towards the final curtain.

The Debut Performance

Performing is an integral part of a dancer's training. No point in being a star in the studio if you can't deliver on the stage. And so, from our very first years at ballet school, young dancers learn to deal with the excitement and the nerves of performing in public through summer specials or end-of-term shows.

My first ballet teacher, Janice Sutton, presented summer shows for the holiday season in Skegness. Although the shows were created largely around the older girls, we youngsters hoped for – and sometimes got – smaller parts along the way. Our real focus each year, though, was the series of festivals (often held in end-of-pier theatres, before they all burned down) in which young dancers would compete for engraved trophies and gold, silver and bronze medals against students from schools around the country.

These early performances were probably more stressful for our parents than they were for us. They had to get us there and back, sometimes a round trip of hundreds of miles on the same day, and make sure we were ready on time, fed, watered, made-up and costumed in outfits handmade, usually, by our mothers. At my peak, I was entered in fourteen different categories at Cleethorpes Festival and my mother made the costume I wore in each of them. I still have my first tutu, lovingly stitched and then altered to make it last one more year.

Sometimes we'd be dancing several numbers over the course of one day – ballet, tap, modern, acrobatics, song and dance, groups, duets and trios. 'Dance nicely,' my father would always say, before joining the other parents to watch helplessly from out front as we went through our routines and then crocodiled on to the stage, all in a line, to await the judges' verdict. And then, when it was all over, they'd wipe away the tears and tell us that there was always next year, load us and our costumes back into the car and let us sleep all the way home. They deserved medals of their own.

At White Lodge, there were performance opportunities too. I might have missed out on *The Nutcracker* in my first year at the school, but it came round with seasonal regularity and two years later, along with eleven other girls from my class and the one below, I finally made it. As a rat. Aged thirteen, and we were performing with The Royal Ballet at Covent Garden, alongside the dancers I'd admired every Christmas in the pages of my *Princess Tina Ballet Annuals*: Lesley Collier, Merle Park, Rudolf Nureyev and Lynn Seymour. Being a rat meant shorter holidays, as *Nutcracker* performances were scattered throughout the Christmas period, but this was a small price to pay. It was our first taste of life with the professionals.

We learned our parts in advance, at White Lodge, and then, as the opening night approached, travelled up to Covent Garden to slot in with the company, where we were allocated underground dressing-rooms alongside the canteen. Our meals, however, came up with us from White Lodge, in big cardboard boxes: Kia-Ora orange juice, sandwiches wrapped in paper and Tunnock's caramel wafer bars. I remember missing the dress rehearsal, lying prone on a tired red velvet banquette in the windowless room, food poisoning frustrating my ambitions, and putting the cardboard boxes to good, if unpleasant, use. I might have missed the dress rehearsal, but I made the first night.

The rats in *The Nutcracker* appear in Clara's nightmare, towards the end of Act I. By defeating the rats and dispatching their King, the Nutcracker wins Clara's heart and together they are whisked away to Act II and the Kingdom of Sweets, where they watch a stream of variations, each of national character, and a *grand pas de deux* before it all falls away and Clara wakes from her dream, safely back home.

In 1976, the company was dancing Rudolf Nureyev's version of *The Nutcracker*, and we rat children worked alongside rat 'parents', dancers from the *corps de ballet*. We came on first, though, from various hiding places around the set, from behind tables, from under the stairs and out of the grandfather clock's belly as it chimed the midnight hour. I was the second rat to appear, charged with the responsibility for counting a pause of four beats and then hitting the second chime exactly on the nose – much harder than the first one, which rolls neatly off the end of a phrase of music. It was a task I took extremely seriously.

Our demise at the end of the scene came in the shape of Quality Street chocolates, fired by the Nutcracker's soldiers from their cannons. Death by chocolate, before any pudding chef dreamed up the name. It wouldn't be allowed these days, or at least they'd have to make sure it was only the soft centres that were loaded into the cannon. A few years ago I came across some of these thirty-year-old sweets, squirrelled away in a chocolate tin full of keepsakes, alongside copies of my end-of-term ballet reports.

Along with the annual summer performances at a theatre local to White Lodge – Richmond, or Wimbledon – these glimpses of their children in *The Nutcracker* offered a rare opportunity for our parents to watch us in action. The only other chance, in those days, was the graduation class, at the end of the fifth form. Seeing their offspring perform at the Royal Opera House, just two years after we had all joined the school, was too good to miss and most of our parents managed, somehow, to get hold of tickets. My sister went along to the box office in person and picked up some hard-to-come-by returns: four tickets in the orchestra stalls, row F, for 12 January 1977.

It was only a few days after we'd all been delivered back to school, post-Christmas holidays, but my parents duly made yet another eight-hour round trip to London to watch *The Nutcracker* and to keep their eyes peeled, as instructed, for the second rat to appear, from behind the grandfather clock. If they caught sight of me at that point, they would have lost me soon afterwards: we were all dressed identically, head-to-toe brown fur with heavy, whiskered masks obscuring our identity. But none of that mattered: it was their first trip to Covent Garden, and their daughter was dancing with The Royal Ballet. When my mum died a few years ago, I found the programme, filed away along with every other printed reference to me that ever appeared, anywhere. I should imagine the village never heard the last of it.

Dancing Together

By the time a young dancer officially joins the *corps de ballet*, some seven or eight years after first arriving at professional school, she is probably relatively relaxed about being on stage, what with *The Nut-cracker*, the annual summer performances and then frequently standing in for company members during the graduate year. That's not to say there are never any butterflies dancing in *corps de ballet* stomachs before the show begins but the *corps*, of necessity, tends to have a relatively pragmatic attitude to performance. If a company performs eight shows in a week (as it might, on tour) the *corps* will be dancing at every one of them. Not for them the fear that this could be the only chance they will get: in five years in the *corps*, a dancer might well perform each role seventy, eighty or a hundred times.

The role the *corps* is dancing when the curtain goes up is probably the first of three or four its dancers will inhabit, along with a corresponding number of costumes, over the course of the evening. Depending on the ballet, they might be required to switch between salt-of-the-earth peasant and otherworldly nymph, or stand-aloof courtier and come-and-get-me whore, with nothing more than a twenty-minute interval and a different outfit to help. Some of the changes (from Peasant to Swan, for instance, in the first act of *Swan Lake*) are too quick to permit a trip back to the dressing-room and so they take place on the side of the stage, in a 'quick-change room' specially constructed each night for this brief, five-minute flurry of dressing and undressing.

The motto of a *corps de ballet* dancer, like a boy scout, could well be 'Be Prepared'. Once the curtain goes up, there is no time for faffing around. Best to have the next headdress and any change of shoes laid out ready and a needle, for emergencies, pre-loaded with thread. Wise, too, to have water and a banana on standby: with costume, shoes and hair to change between (and sometimes during) acts, there's barely time to go to the loo, let alone visit the canteen.

It may all be busy-busy and, at times, a bit repetitive, but there is something very satisfying about being part of a great *corps de ballet*. It is, literally, the *body* of the company, its backbone. Without a strong *corps de ballet*, you don't really have a company. The *corps* holds the performance together, weaving a thread between the solos and the *pas de deux*. It sets the scene and the style. And the *corps de ballet* supports the principals, in every sense: Giselle's fellow villagers are her friends, both in the story and for real. If she needs them they will be there, offering an encouraging smile, a rallying 'you can do it' whispered at just the right moment, or a helpful reminder of where Giselle is supposed to go in those group sections she's never had the chance to rehearse with the rest of the cast. And of course the *corps de ballet*'s own dances provide much needed breathing space for the principals, between their entrances, solos and *pas de deux*.

So what makes a good *corps*? A good *corps* is one that not only moves together, it even thinks alike. Its dancers respond to music in a similar way and they understand the *répétiteurs*' shorthand without explanation, saving time and limiting mistakes. If the majority of the dancers in the *corps de ballet* have been trained in the same school, they share an understanding of basic positions, style, repertoire and traditions – as well as the company culture – but nowadays, this is rarely the case. EU employment law combined with cheap air travel mean that dancers can and do travel to find work and so a twenty-first-century *corps de ballet* is likely to include upwards of a dozen nationalities. With this much diversity inherent in the group, perhaps the only point of commonality among the *corps*, aside from talent, is the dancers' incredible discipline.

I don't think I realised, until I stopped dancing, just how deep that discipline runs. In the company, we didn't credit ourselves as being particularly disciplined: we were just doing our job. But it's a job that demands a level of self-control that many people would find challenging, if not impossible: working silently, with eleven, twenty-three, or thirty-one other dancers, to create the impression of a body moving as one; watching sideways, forwards and backwards at the same time and being ready to adapt your timing, position or placing without complaint; standing stock still, after four or five minutes of demanding choreography, resisting the urge to fidget even when the calf muscle of the supporting leg is threatening to explode; learning and remembering five or six ballets in any one month and rehearsing them day in, day out; keeping quiet when the version you remember is overruled and you're forced to do something you're convinced is incorrect; twelve-hour days, on your feet, six days a week. And, on occasion, it involves finishing one show only to start it all over again, with less than a two-hour break between curtain-down and curtain-up.

It is this discipline, allied to the mutual desire to create a great show, that allows the *corps de ballet* to continue to work effectively, even in the twenty-first century. If *The Red Shoes* is to be believed (and there's no reason it shouldn't, chiming as it does with autobiographies and first-hand reports of the same period), the *corps de ballets* of yesteryear functioned largely through fear, with the director or ballet mistress exercising some kind of *in loco parentis* control. This was not necessarily out of kilter with expectations of working life in the wider population. Respect for one's elders and 'betters', for institutions and authority, were a given. Young people didn't expect to have their opinions and feelings taken into account.

Over the last twenty years all this has changed: some time during the 1980s and 1990s, the demand for individual rights overtook a sense of collective responsibility and the search for self-fulfilment replaced the quest for the common good. But still great *corps de ballets* exist (making a nonsense of the complaint that young people these days have no discipline, no respect for tradition and no ability to concentrate for longer than thirty seconds). They do so because a group of dancers makes an active choice to subjugate individuality to a shared cause: creating the extraordinary effects possible when a body of dancers works as one.

Of course, it's not always harmony and concord. No dancer joins the *corps de ballet* hoping to stay there: we all want our time in the *corps* to be just the first rung on a ladder that goes all the way to the top. Frustration at the pace of your own upwards trajectory, or resentment at someone else's, can lead to tension in the ranks. The diaries of my first two years in the company record all this as I struggled to make any sort of mark, my mood flip-flopping between hopeless gloom and indignant rage and my favourite entry particularly terse: 17 September 1983, *'As for my career – my what?'*

Some dancers make the choice at this point to try their luck elsewhere and audition for alternative companies where the repertoire (or the director) is a better match with their qualities and skills, but this involves converting what may be a childhood dream – at White Lodge, we all hoped to make it in The Royal Ballet – into an adult ambition. Others stick it out, either because they aren't ready to give up on the dream or, more rationally, because a new director or resident choreographer might be on the horizon. Besides, on the basis that everything changes – ironically, one of the few things on which you can rely – there's always room for optimism.

But however much you might be itching for the promotion that takes you out of it, you never forget your time in the *corps de ballet*. It's hard work and it's constant but it's also great fun. On tour as *corps de ballet* members, in Asia, Europe or America, we saw everything and went everywhere, soaking up new continents and cultures. So what if we were a bit tired from all that sightseeing? We knew we'd be able to deliver a good show and, besides, it wasn't us in the spotlight. In later years, the responsibilities of principal status made me much more cautious. Sightseeing had to be carefully timed: I couldn't risk the heavy legs that followed a day spent walking around Japan's shrines or New York's museums and galleries.

While you sometimes feel like a hamster on a wheel, with *Sleeping Beauties* and *Swan Lakes* all merging into one never-ending performance in which you're destined, for ever, to play no more than a supporting role, every so often – a world premiere, an auspicious debut, the retirement of a star – a show comes along to remind you just what a privileged position you hold, even if that position is a lowly spot on the end of the back row. But what really stands out, at least for me, is the sense of camaraderie and togetherness and I realise now that it is this, more than anything, that sets the *corps de ballet* years apart.

The time spent in the *corps* is the only time in a dancer's life when dancing is not, in essence, a solitary business. Throughout all those years of training – despite the fact that 'class' always takes place amid a mass of other dancers – your struggles and your achievements are yours, and yours alone. Later on, in solo and principal roles, you will stand or fall by your own efforts. But a *corps de ballet* can triumph only if each and every dancer succeeds at the same time. 'Greater than the sum of its parts' could have been coined to describe a great *corps*.

Dancing Alone

At some point during those first few years in the company, if your potential has been noted, you'll find yourself cast to dance your first solo. Ideally, the moment will come within a year or two of joining the company: the longer you wait, the harder it becomes. A speedy ascent into solo roles is not just satisfying in terms of career progression; there are practical advantages, too. A year or so after graduation, you're likely to have retained much of the peak fitness you acquired as a student, when you were dancing flat out, six or seven hours a day. (*Corps de ballet* life can be a bit of a shock after this: in the early days, as a cover, you might spend more hours watching rehearsals from the sidelines, waiting your turn, than you spend dancing.) During your last year in the school, you'll have danced many of the solos from the classics as part of the curriculum – and you might even have performed a principal role at your graduation performance – so dancing alone will still feel relatively familiar.

Typically, the first solo you're cast to dance will be both short and well known, something you've learned at school or watched over and over again from your place at the side of the stage: one of the many variations in *The Sleeping Beauty* (Fairies in the Prologue,

Jewels, Cats or Red Riding Hood in Act III), the *pas de trois* or Neapolitan in *Swan Lake* or the Peasant *pas* in the first act of *Giselle*. With three or four dancers ahead of you on the cast list, you might get just one scheduled performance: at most, it will be two.

Chances are it will be the matinee of a double-show day and so you'll dance your debut *pas de trois* plus Cygnets in the afternoon and then your normal roster of Peasants, Swans and Czardas at night. You'll have been in the theatre until 11 o'clock the night before and arrived early the next morning, less than twelve hours later. If it's a Saturday matinee – the conventional show for trying out new casts – it will be the end of a working week and you'll probably be exhausted before you start. There is little time for nerves as you step out alone on the stage for the first time as a fully-fledged professional dancer, chosen – you can hardly believe it – at last.

For some dancers the first solo role comes not in the nineteenth-century classics but in something more recent. The repertoire of most ballet companies includes a mixture of full-length ballets (generally three acts) as well as mixed bills made up of (usually three) one-act pieces. With at least six soloist and principal roles (and sometimes more than that) on offer, these mixed bills provide a perfect opportunity, within a run of performances, for the company director to try out younger, less experienced dancers.

It was in one of these mixed bills that I found

myself elevated from my place in the *corps* to dance two performances of the first *pas de trois* in Balanchine's *Agon*. It wasn't a conventional route out of the *corps*, but it felt to me like a good place to start, the costume (black leotard and pink tights) the everyday dancer's regular attire, the choreography a witty inversion of the classical technique that, by then, I knew so well.

Occasionally, debuts are unscheduled, or come at very short notice indeed. A ballet company's cast sheet, particularly in the big classics, is like a series of ifs and buts, with younger dancers cast in multiple roles and covering several more. It takes only one dancer to be injured for the carefully constructed casting to tumble like a deck of cards: an injured ankle forces tomorrow's Aurora to cancel and the Lilac Fairy is asked to step up. So the Crystal Fountain Fairy becomes Lilac, Woodland Glade becomes Crystal Fountain and, five cast changes later, a Court Lady gets her first solo. If a dancer is injured once the curtain has gone up, the alternative casts might already have left the theatre and there will be no option but to find a costume for the cover and send her on.

I danced my first Gamzatti in *La Bayadère* a week or so earlier than expected, when Darcey Bussell slipped and fell during the first act. I had been out front watching, but less than ten minutes after her fall I was on stage for the coda. Viviana Durante wasn't even a cover for Odette/Odile when she replaced Maria Almeida, halfway through a performance of *Swan Lake*. She learned it live, with her partner, Jay Jolley, talking her through the steps as they performed.

Sometimes, but very rarely, with so many possible combinations of role and casting, dancers miss their name on the notice board and go home early, leaving a gap on stage. And so it was at very short notice – two or three minutes – that I once found myself dancing two roles - the Jewels trio and the Bluebirds – in a single performance of *The Sleeping Beauty*.

Principals, Stand by on Stage, Please

While the *corps de ballet* dances away on stage, the stars of the show await their moment in the wings, pacing, jogging, stretching, fixing ribbons, repinning hair, visualising, breathing deep. For the *corps* and some of the soloists, it might be just another fixture in a long run of shows, but there is nothing matter-of-fact about this performance for tonight's principals. However many times you might have danced a role, however comfortable you are in its challenges, however acclaimed your interpretation, for a principal dancer there is never really a time at which performance becomes routine.

That's not to say that all dancers are necessarily nervous before they perform. Some remain totally unfazed by the pressure; others struggle to retain any sense of calm. Most veer between the two, depending on the ballet. If a role is familiar, or one to which your physique, technique and temperament are best suited, the feeling is likely to be of nervous excitement, of potential waiting to be fulfilled. Less familiar roles, or roles in which you're ill at ease, seem to alter your relationship with your legs, making the ground beneath your feet that much less stable.

'Nerves' (as opposed to nervous excitement) take over when the demands of the role exceed your belief in your ability to cope and this can happen for any number of reasons: ill health, injury, exhaustion, a bad review, an overheard bitchy comment undermining your self-esteem. In some roles, the ghosts of previous years hover in the wings and, try as you might, it's very hard not to be conscious of the long shadow in which you perform.

Your own childhood dreams may be haunting you, too. These are the ballets you aspired to long before you knew any others. Seeing your name in the printed programme should be the fulfilment of those dreams and, if life were a film, the end credits would be rolling as you made your first entrance – as they did in *Billy Elliot*. But this is for real. Being cast, if and when it happens, is not the end of the fairy tale. It's just the beginning of another story.

So the dancer waiting in the wings might well be pacing up and down as she awaits her entrance. It could be in an effort to keep warm, or it could be because she's finding it hard to stand still. Sometimes it's hard to tell.

About five minutes before her cue to go on, you'll notice a change in focus. As the *corps de ballet* starts into the waltz that marks her standby, she bends over to make final checks on her shoes and then reaches up to repin a section of her hair. Leg warmers are peeled off and put to one side and she takes another slug of water from her bottle, rolling it around her mouth before swallowing it down.

With both hands holding her right hip in place, she twists her upper body forcefully to the right. There's a muffled clunk as the lower spine releases its tension. Each leg is hoisted high above her head and then, with her hands clasped together and turned inside out, she pulls both arms forwards, rounding her back to stretch out her upper spine. Shoulders are circled, first one way and then the other. Four or five quick *relevés* activate her feet and ankles and warm the calves. Then, pulling each heel in turn up behind her towards her tutu, she stretches out the muscles along the front of her thighs. Jogging on the spot, she shakes her hands furiously, as if to rid them of water, but it's tension she's trying to shake off. The music on stage is coming to a climax and she's about to go on.

Somewhere in among all this activity she might remind herself that this moment is what she's trained for: it's what she has wanted for at least fifteen years.

On stage, the entire cast turns to face the upstage

corner where, any moment now, she'll make her entrance. The crotchets reduce to quavers, and then semiquavers, as the notes ascend the scale. There's no going back now, despite the knot in her stomach. Her shoes aren't quite right and she's seized by a sudden, desperate urge to go to the loo. Too late now. She's not going anywhere, except on to the stage. It's the music that eventually pulls her on and suddenly, she's there: centre stage and the centre of attention.

The first entrance is light, fast and very short, skittering from one side to the other and then back to the upstage corner. No matter then that her feet on the ground don't feel quite stable: in this blithe little sequence, she's not on them for long enough to notice. One more diagonal and then it ends as soon as it's started, spinning across the stage to a static pose. (Arms slightly forward of the head: we're in the nineteenth century now.)

It's like being fired from a starter pistol and as she holds the final position her heart pounds, both with the sudden exertion and the awareness of what's to come. She remembers to close her mouth. She's about to launch into one of the most famous of all dances, a dance by which ballerinas have been measured for over a hundred years. Around the stage, her colleagues look on expectantly and, out front, the audience settles after a brief volley of applause. The regulars know that the entrance was but an *entrée*: the main course is about to begin.

It's easy to be overwhelmed on stage by the expectations attached to this particular dance, the famous balances overshadowing its beautiful structure and its eloquent choreography. She knows this and is determined not to allow it, focusing instead on the music – the gorgeous ebb and flow of Tchaikovsky – and on the interaction with her four Cavaliers. The hurdles will come but, for now, it's a dance of self-discovery as she meets not only her four potential suitors but also the first stirrings within her of the woman she will become.

One by one, she greets her partners, each touch a regal handshake, her demeanour demure and her leg raised only so high that it doesn't distort the line of the tutu's skirt. She has just this one brief sequence across the front of the stage in which to steady her heartbeat before she must walk around and prepare for the first of those fiendish balances. The regulars in the audience are keen to see how she'll manage. Some of her fellow dancers have their doubts. She's trying to stay focused. In the studio, they are so, so easy but here on the stage, with costumes, lights, a full house and, most of all, her own self-doubt, they are elusive, hard to land. It's as if reality has slipped out of alignment and no part of her body is quite where it's supposed to be. In the studio she can step into *attitude* and know exactly where to find the point of balance. Now, she feels a bit drunk.

The first partner saves her, his hand steady as a rock. She needs to lean on the music, to let it drive her, to follow its cue in releasing her grip so that the next Cavalier can step in, but it's like trying to dive off the high board. The courage won't come and the music is dancing on. Around the stage they're holding their collective breath and willing her to do it – it's no fun watching a dancer fail at this point, with two more acts to go. With nothing more than blind faith to rely on, she lets go, then again, then again, and the first set is over. Not triumphant, but not disastrous either. The stage breathes out, the music goes on.

Back in the dressing-room between acts, it's important not to focus on what went wrong and what might have been. There'll be time for that tomorrow but, for now, the only way to look is forward, to the next act and the next challenge.

Sometimes, the *répétiteur* will come backstage at this point, with a few words of encouragement or congratulation, depending on how it's gone. This is the one person who really understands what you were trying to achieve, who noticed the little triumphs that will have passed the audience by: that you managed to keep your shoulders down, or your arms forward, or your mouth closed. These tiny achievements (often the erosion of bad habits ingrained over twenty years) can allow you to feel triumphant even when the party tricks went awry.

With around twenty-five minutes to go before the next act begins, there isn't too much time to recover and prepare. The wig mistress comes back to change the headdress and tidy up any stray ends. You add powder and fresh lipstick, replace a plaster, change into the next pair of shoes and then, as the tannoy announces the five-minute call, the dresser comes in to help you into the costume for the next act. The atmosphere in the dressing-room is noticeably less tense than it was at the half. The first – and the biggest – hurdle is over.

In most ballets, the choreography builds in intensity towards the last act but tonight the toughest bit is over within the first ten minutes on stage. There's even space for a joke and some light-hearted banter, but it doesn't quite ring true. The hard part may be over, but there are still two more acts to go before the final curtain.

10.30 Curtain Down

Three hours after it first swept up into the proscenium arch, the red velvet curtain sweeps back down again as the closing bars sound out from the pit. The principals, wrapped in each other's arms for the ballet's final *tableau*, slip out of character, their stage embrace converted to a genuine hug as they celebrate a job well done, or share their disappointment in a performance that never quite took off. The orchestra's final notes are lost to the stage, muffled behind the thick fabric of the drapes and buried beneath the beginnings of the audience's applause.

On stage, reality rushes back in. Two assistant stage managers hurry on from the wings to catch the heavy tabs as they meet, intent on preventing them from bouncing open again to reveal a muddle of dancers scurrying into lines for the calls. The stage manager chivvies things along: 'Quick as you can, please, full call' – but nobody's keen to drag this out. The audience's applause may be hard earned, but we're also aware that it's voluntary; we don't want to push our luck when we know they have trains to catch and homes to get back to.

Generally, the calls begin with a full company line-up: principals in the middle, with the leading soloist roles either side of them, status diminishing as distance from the centre increases. Depending on the ballet, there may be a second line, directly behind, of less significant solo or featured roles. At the back, in a row of their own, are the dancers of the *corps de ballet*. Neighbours' hands are held, up and down the lines. 'Forward and back, please,' comes the instruction from the stage manager. The lines advance as a block, taking their pace from the principals. Down by the footlights, the ballerina acknowledges the audience, one hand still holding her partner's, the other stretched out in a gesture that takes in the entire theatre. She curtsies, deep, her hand now clasped in towards her heart. Her partner bows. The lines of dancers echo their moves, a little more prosaic, a little less self-aware. Backing up, the dancers in the character roles – usually heavily costumed and wigged – may have to manipulate a long train to ensure they don't walk backwards up their own costume, bringing themselves to their knees.

Flowers – from friends, fans and family – are brought on stage for the principal dancer and for two or three of the soloists. A young dancer in a debut solo receives far more bouquets than the dancer playing the lead, which may be confusing for newcomers in the audience, who generally assume the flowers are standard issue, paid for by the theatre's management. It never feels quite right to put these flowers on the floor, and so there follows a moment of confusion while the recipients try to work out how to continue to hold the hands of the dancers alongside them as well as two hard-to-grasp bouquets. To add to the challenge, the stage manager calls out, 'Conductor, please', and the ballerina goes to the downstage wing to bring him on, a much needed hand reluctantly released from the flower juggling to reach out and greet him. He kisses the hand and then heads straight downstage to indicate his orchestra. The dancers move forward to join him, the principals this time echoing his gesture towards the musicians in the pit, before the entire company retreats upstage as the tabs come in.

After the full calls comes a line-up of the *corps de ballet* alone – 'Stand on the right, no, the right,' one dancer hisses, determined that the precision for which this *corps* is renowned is maintained right to the very end – followed by the 'red runners', in which the various characters, soloists and principals go through barely parted tabs to take a bow in front of the curtain.

Sometimes, a second red cloth would come down behind the curtains so that the crew could get on with clearing the set, safely out of view, while the dancers continued the calls. 'King, Queen and Catalabutte, mind your 'eads, please', rang out from the stage manager as the red runners for *Sleeping Beauty* began, reminding us in a single sentence of both the first artists to go through the tabs and the need to stand clear of the heavy cloth descending.

With the red runners under way, the *corps de ballet* is released, officially off duty for the first time since

10.30. It's the end of a long day, a day that started twelve hours earlier and that will be repeated, *Ground-hog*-style, in twelve hours' time. And it's not over yet: they have still to warm down, get out of costume and make-up, remove wigs, shower and travel home.

The orchestra's players, by now, are back in the band room, packing up their instruments and changing out of their blacks. The stage crew stands by to strike the set or, if it's the last performance of the run, to start the 'get-out', which sees the production packed up and sent off to storage until it next comes back into the repertoire. For the majority of the two hundred or so people involved in delivering this single perform-ance, it's just another good day's work, well done.

For the principals, though, curtain-down repre-sents something more significant. If curtain-up is the ultimate deadline – unarguable, unforgiving and unavoidable – curtain-down might well be the ulti-mate example of closure. With one sweep of the cur-tain, years of wanting, months of preparation and a few hours of hard work are brought to their conclu-sion. It's a complex feeling, relief that it's over (and that you got through with dignity relatively intact) mixing with a sense of loss that the moment and all its potential is gone, a *petite mort*, triumph (perhaps) tinged with *tristesse*.

The endless possibilities that filled the empty stage at the moment the curtain went up have been reduced to one reality and, no matter how good that reality turned out to be, there is still a sense of mourning for all the possibilities that will never now become real. It's the same sensation I felt as a child, each Christmas morning: however satisfying the presents contained within my sack, the reality never quite matched the heady thrill of imagining what it might contain.

But there is no time to reflect on this, not at this point. As soon as the curtains close on the ballet's final moment, the stage manager is hustling the principals to join the calls, standing by to cue the tabs the moment you're settled in place. The tabs sweep up, the volume of applause increases and, for the first time in the evening, you look out at the audience not as a character, not even as a dancer, but as you.

It's one of the questions I'm most often asked and one of the hardest to answer: what is it like to be applauded by a theatre full of people? It's certainly humbling, and a privilege, to experience this public appreciation of everything you achieved. Most people have to wait for their own funeral to enjoy this kind of tribute. But while that's all true, it's not complete. I wonder now whether it's hard to describe the moment because we are never fully present within it, and whether absenting a part of oneself is a way of dealing with all that attention.

Dancers' personalities are not entirely extrovert, despite the way it may seem. Many of us are happy to be in the spotlight when we are working, but not, if we're not. Curtain calls fall uncomfortably between the two states. Conventions vary across different companies, but I was always taught that curtain calls should not be taken in character – with true 'character' roles – Widow Simone in *La Fille Mal Gardée*, for instance, or Von Rothbart in *Swan Lake* – the exceptions to this. So in curtain calls a dancer is working, yes, but without the protection of the role you've been playing for the last two or three hours. Suddenly, with no time at all to make the transition, you're the wrong side of the curtain, playing yourself.

The final calls – the prince alone in front of the curtain, then the ballerina, before she calls him back for one more bow – have a particular intensity. Now, you're right down by the footlights, level with the proscenium arch. You're closer to the audience than ever, in every sense. No role to hide behind and just a foot or so of stage between you and a pit now silent and empty. When the curtain is up, the music that emanates from the pit's dark depths is both a protective barrier and your most reliable support; now it has nothing to offer, its chairs abandoned, the musical scores on each stand all turned to the final page. For these few minutes, there is nothing between you – the real you – and the audience.

These moments are the hardest of all to rationalise.

The warmth is genuine, the affection real; there may be flowers raining down from the gallery and people standing on their feet refusing to leave, even though the house lights are up and the exit doors ajar. But you still don't want to believe it, not quite, because, in the words of a friend, still very much a star: 'If you do, you may start to take yourself more seriously than you take your work. And you don't want to do that.'

Eventually, the applause dies away and the tabs are closed for the last time. The company director and a small group of the ballet staff have come backstage via the pass door from their seats out front and they're making their way towards you, centre stage. The *corps de ballet* is long gone and the soloists have drifted off towards the dressing-rooms, too. The high-octane nervous energy of the performance is fast ebbing away, replaced by something more pragmatic, more practical. All around, the carefully constructed artifice – palace, forest or lake – is being dismantled and inside you, too, the person you are is overtaking the character you've been.

It's like that moment at the end of a party, when harsh overhead lighting replaces the fairy lights and the candles so that the washing-up can be tackled, the carpet vacuumed and normality restored. With one click of a switch the magic of the blues and the dim and the half-lights exists only in the memory. The remaining two dancers feel suddenly rather small and vulnerable on a big, empty stage; the immunity of performance – nobody, as far as I'm aware, is ever hassled by their bank manager while the curtain is up – is stripped away.

The two dancers collect up their tracksuits, leg warmers and water bottles from corners of the stage and juggle to keep them, and the bouquets of flowers, aloft. Hugs are exchanged as well as polite thanks, to each other and to the staff who prepared them for the roles. There might be kisses and congratulations, there might be corrections and consolations but the tone, if possible, will remain positive. Tomorrow is the moment for the post-show post-mortem, should one be needed, and, besides, the ballet staff all know what it's like to perform. If it's not gone well, there is nothing anyone can say that will help you feel better about it.

Back in the dressing-room: surrounded now by dis-carded shoes, balled-up tissues and the contents of the hairpin box (emptied out earlier, in the search for a missing ear-ring), with four bunches of Cellophane-wrapped flowers piled into the sink. It's already 10.45 and the dresser is keen to get you out of your costume (and herself, understandably, out of the building). Now that they're off, you're aware of the kid gloves that everyone around you was wearing earlier, how visible your nerves must have been. Now, it's all chatty good humour, pot shots at the impossible schedule and 'What are you doing on Sunday?' The dresser hangs the last of your costumes on the rail behind your place and heads off, calling out as she goes one more 'Well done', possibly the last you'll hear tonight. You wrap up in a fleece and sit down to take off your shoes. A few dancers pass along the corridor outside and then it all falls silent. You snip away at the stitches holding the ribbons in place and untie first the right and then the left. Over the tannoy, you can hear the sounds of the set being dismantled on stage but, aside from that, it seems as if you're the only person left in the theatre right now.

You ease off one shoe and then the other, spreading and stretching your toes into their new-found freedom. Men will never be able to understand the exquisitely delightful sensation of removing *pointe* shoes after a three-act ballet, but any woman who has worn too-high heels ('car-to-bar' shoes) to a stand-up party will be some way towards recognising the feeling. Agony as the blood finds its way back into the bits it had deserted; gorgeous, blessed relief a moment later, as sensation returns. With toes free and wiggling again, it's time to stretch – calves, hamstrings, thighs – to help remove the lactic acid from the muscles and improve the way you'll feel in the morning. To be honest, it's the last thing you want to do at this time of night but, the older you get, the harder it becomes to take shortcuts with your body.

The carefully constructed make-up and hair are rapidly dismantled, like the set. Busy fingers delve into the curls of the wig, locating pins and pulling them out, even as the other hand continues the search. A pile builds up on the dressing-table, like an abandoned game of pick-up sticks: restoring order in the hairpin box can wait for tomorrow. Cottonwool soaked in surgical spirit helps to dissolve the glue that is sticking the wig to your temples and cheekbones but, in the end, you'll have to take a deep breath and rip it off (and a micro-layer of your skin, too). The wig goes back in its box, but with less care than it came out. It will be dressed again for next time, if there is one.

A fist full of Nivea, rubbed all over the face, takes care of everything but the heavy-duty mascara, which will respond only to neat baby oil. For a moment, a panda stares back from the mirror before tissues wipe it all away and a pale-faced, dark-circles-under-the-eyes version of yourself comes into view. One pair of shoes is shellac-ed, in the hope that they will dance another day; a second is thrown into a pile earmarked for the bin, once ribbons have been removed to be reused.

The cards attached to the flowers are read and then added to the selection tucked under the mirror's frame, a reminder, for when it's needed, that there are people out there who care. Tights and knickers go into the bag on their way home to the washing machine. Then a shower, the hot water washing away the sweat, the last vestiges of make-up and the aching muscles. It took around three hours to get ready for the show: by five past eleven you're wrapping plastic bags around the wet stalks of the flowers, balancing them across one arm, picking up your bag and heading out of the door.

The corridors have the same air of between times that you encountered on the way in. The crew, as before, is working on the stage. The offices are empty now, the cleaning team yet to arrive. The shutter of the coffee bar is down. You check the notice board on the way out – it's a golden rule. You can never assume that nothing has changed in the hours since you came in. Perhaps a dancer was injured during the show, and there's an emergency rehearsal tomorrow to slot in a new cast. It may not affect you directly, but it could impact on studio space, or on the *répétiteur* who was scheduled to work with you at the same time.

At the stage door, there may be friends or family waiting, people who've seen the show. If it's been a good one, this is extremely welcome: not only does it prolong the moment of celebration, it's practical, too. You need to eat and you're likely to be experiencing a kind of euphoria that will last well into the night. Going out for a meal will address both issues – there's no point lying in bed, wide awake and pretending you might get to sleep, even when you know you're due back at work in about eleven hours' time.

If you're disappointed with the way the show turned out, you have a choice: bail out of any social arrangements and head home to lick your wounded self-esteem over a bowl of pasta, or endure an uncomfortable hour or so while your friends try to find positive things to say and you try to remember it's not the end of the world.

Outside the stage door, there's a small group of loyal fans waiting, as well as some less familiar faces, with programmes and photographs to be signed. The loyal fans could be your sternest critics – after all, they are regular attenders who clock up almost as many shows as the ballet staff, so they're well placed to compare your performance against everyone else's, and against everything else you've ever done. But in truth they are almost always generous in their praise, at least for the dancers. Repertoire choices, casting and the general 'state of the dancing nation' are frequently up for healthy debate.

I'm sure most companies have this kind of dedicated fan base, a group of people who care passionately about the company and about its dancers, who delight in spotting a young artist from within the *corps* and then tracking and supporting her progress through the roles and the ranks. Early on, it's a boost to morale to be spotted in this way, particularly if the roles and promotions are slow to come. Later on, the fans' reliable presence at the stage door, and the support it implies, feels steadying and constant in a career that doesn't offer much in the way of sureties.

The image of the dancer leaving the theatre alone – muffled up against the cold, weighed down with flowers and bags, face pale, hair stiff with spray, and struggling to negotiate the ticket barrier at Covent Garden tube station – is probably not the picture most people have of a ballerina but, for the everyday dancer, this is what it's like. Yes, on occasion, there are after-show parties, dinners and taxis home, but you're more likely to find us in the 24-hour Tesco picking up a pint of milk than you are to catch us in Boujis or China White. It's home as quickly as possible, dinner, washing machine on, emails, television or radio, and off to bed.

In the movies, it's not like this. In the movies, the cast heads off to a glamorous opening-night party after curtain-down and steadily drinks champagne until the morning papers bring news of the show's fate. But Covent Garden is not Broadway: the only all-nighters are the ones worked by the crew, striking the set, and the critics don't play quite the same role in closing shows, at least not overnight. When I was dancing, the first review to appear was usually in London's evening paper, the newspaper with the increasingly truncated title: *London Evening Standard*, *Evening Standard* and then, finally, the *Standard*. (I was fully expecting it to go one further and become *Stan*.)

The *Standard* appeared on the news-stands around 4 o'clock, just about the time we were making the trip between the rehearsal studios in West London and the Royal Opera House in Covent Garden. Full of nervous trepidation, we'd buy a copy and read it on the tube, flicking through the pages towards the back (reviews are generally hidden somewhere towards the rear of the papers, between the obituaries and the small ads) with the same horrified fascination passers-by display at the scene of an accident. You can't look, but you can't look away.

There is a similar contradiction in our feelings towards the critics and the conclusions they reach. If the review is good, we're likely to think we pulled the wool over their eyes, that we 'got away with it'. If it's bad, it confirms our worst suspicions about ourselves, making public our deepest and most private fears. And even the most intelligent, articulate and persuasive writer is going to have a hard job competing with our own internal critic, which is likely to be forever disappointed with our own performances.

Looking back now at the files of cuttings I kept (and the crates full my mother managed to amass) I'm amazed at the things people wrote about me, and my performances, down the years. I may have read them when they were published, but I'm *seeing* them now for the first time. If only I'd been able to appreciate fully their lovely compliments, they might have gone some way to eroding the ever present dancer's self-doubt I carried with me. But of course it's a catch 22 (or should that be a 'catch tutu'?): it's that same self-doubt which prevents the praise from hitting its mark.

The Final Curtain

The everyday nature of what we do is another of the oddities of a dancer's life. Every night the curtain comes down and the next morning we're back at the *barre* again: another day, another set of *pliés*. It can fool you into thinking that life is like this, that there will always be another chance to try again to get it right. And then, at some point, the curtain comes down for the very last time and the final smattering of applause fades away. It's the same sense of emptiness and mourning that comes after every performance, but this time it's for more than just the possibilities that never were. It's for everything that came to pass but that will never do so again.

I wish I could say that dancers routinely prepare for this moment with the same sort of calculated precision with which we prepare for performance, but this wouldn't, for the most part, be true. Relatively few dancers plan seriously for their transition out of a career that, by its very nature, has obsolescence built in. But it's peopled with Peter Pans, this short and all-consuming career: we all seem so young and retirement always seems so far away. Nobody under the age of twenty really wants to think about pensions, and no young dancer really wants to consider life after the stage.

It's not so much that it's hard to see what we might do next: it's just that it's difficult to envisage a career that will provide as much pleasure, challenge, stimulation and satisfaction as dancing. How many people have the privilege of doing what they love and getting paid for it? So where do you go from there?

Perhaps it's not surprising we struggle to approach career planning with the objectivity an adult might bring to it. For most of us, the decision to dance was a childhood dream pursued into adulthood. At the age of seven, or thereabouts, we fixed our sights on a goal and steered a course towards it, often without any confusing junctions to negotiate along the way. Those of us who graduate from a school into its parent company and then progress up through its ranks can reach a relatively ripe age – thirty-eight, in my case – without having taken a single career decision in our lives.

But, at some point, when the invincibility of youth wears off and you're forced to accept that you won't be dancing for ever, you're presented with a fairly major question: what next, when you've only ever done one thing? The question forms quietly, a half-whispered thought that becomes gently more insistent as the seasons go by.

All sorts of external factors turn up the volume: injury – so easy to shrug off when you were younger – now requires a significant lay-off and a long, slow rehabilitation; a ballet in which you were always first cast comes back into the repertoire but it's been recast entirely with younger dancers; a choreographer who always chose you for his ballets creates something new but this time you're not involved. Your scheduled performances decrease, year on year, making each one unnerving in a way that is unfamiliar to you – there is definitely an inverse relationship between the number of performances you dance and the level of fear that attaches to them. Your place in the busy machine is shifting: no longer a central cog on which many other cogs turn, you're beginning to feel like a spare part – useful to have around, but not exactly essential, except in emergencies.

By this point, you suspect that the 'What next?' question is being asked elsewhere, too – and this is the tricky bit. It's unlikely that your view of 'how long you've got left' matches exactly with the management's. So nobody's keen to admit too publicly that they are thinking ahead to their life beyond dance, lest it prompts their employer to start thinking about it, too. Some dancers are ready for this, with an alternative plan already mapped out but, for many of us, transition remains something around the corner, out of sight, until we find ourselves turning that corner and staring it – and therefore ourselves – in the face.

Since childhood, dancing has been the way we define ourselves, as much who we are as what we do. Night after night, post-performance, we revert easily from a place in the spotlight to a more familiar role as the everyday dancer but the transition post-career – from everyday dancer to everyman or woman – is not so straightforward.

Not all of us are able to identify, for ourselves, the right moment to bring the curtain down on our dancing career and so it is brought down for us. Perhaps it is inevitable, when this is the case, that you neither hear nor heed the warnings. *Tabs coming in. Mind your head.* Except it's not your head that struggles to make sense of it, at least not in my case. I had danced with the company for twenty years, nine of them as a principal. My future had, by then, come forward to meet me and I was busy and challenged doing other things, juggling and enjoying several alternative careers.

If I'm being honest – and I am, now – dancing no longer held me in its grip quite as firmly as it once had. I was performing less and less, and you can't be a part-time ballet dancer at any age – certainly not at the age of thirty-eight. It's just too hard. It was time to move on and my head got it. But, deep inside me,

the young child who had always wanted to be a ballerina did not want to give up. It was somewhere in
my stomach that I felt the blow.

Transitions are always tough: the transition out of a
career that has held you in thrall for much of your
conscious life may be particularly challenging. Not
only does it involve letting go of something you've
held dear since childhood, it also means starting
again, possibly in an entirely new profession, without the benefits of youth on your side. Dancers dance
through what are, undoubtedly, our 'best' years, when
we are at our fittest and most adaptable, when our
brains are at their sharpest. We dance through our
childbearing years and the years when, convention-
ally, we might be working towards a degree.

There is support and advice available, in many
countries, to smooth the process of a dancer's transition, but it's an unavoidable truth that dancers who
enter formal retraining after twenty years in the profession are likely to be forty or more when they finally
emerge on the job market as a first-time employee in
a new career.

On the other hand, a life spent dancing is a surpris-
ingly effective preparation for a second career. Above
and beyond the discipline – that much must be obvious – many of the skills acquired in the studio and

on stage translate effectively into a more conventional workplace: dancers stick rigorously to deadlines and learn early on about performing on demand; they're adept at trying out new ideas (in the studio) and testing them in the market place (for a dancer, the stage), gathering feedback (in the form of applause, good and bad reviews and the teacher's corrections) and applying it all to their next efforts; they learn about leadership – good and bad – on a daily basis, as different teachers try different ways of galvanising a group of dancers who may be half-asleep; they know how to set targets and devise strategies for achieving them, step by step, day by day; they can live with playing the long game – Lord knows, they have to – and they accept that a necessary part of improvement is the discomfort along the way. They know that it's only through failure that you find out what works and what doesn't and they understand the weighty responsibility of tradition as well as the dilemma it presents: too little respect and heritage can be destroyed, too much and the future is at risk.

Looking back, almost a decade after my last performance – and with rose-tinted retrospectacles set to one side – I can see how the ups and downs of a life in dance have shaped who I am: my attitudes, my approach, my values and beliefs. Perhaps anyone who has been a dancer for all those years – through child-hood, adolescence and into adulthood – will always carry a vestige of that remarkable privilege within. Dancing leaves an indelible mark: a profound and literal body of knowledge, distilled from decades in the studio and on the stage; it creates the dancer from the dance.

At the end of the day, it is this that the everyday dancer takes away.

Acknowledgements

I could not have written *The Everyday Dancer* without my many years spent dancing and so profound thanks are due to all those people from whom I learned so much along the way: teachers, *répétiteurs*, choreographers, directors, musicians, physiotherapists, writers and, of course, dancers.

Working on the book, I've been enormously grateful to everyone at Faber, particularly Belinda Matthews (for her patience, kindness and generous advice) and Kate Ward (for wise editorial guidance); to Laurie Lewis, for finding in his files the beautiful image on the cover; to Millicent Hodson, for the lovely line drawings which begin each chapter; to John-Martin White, for the author photograph; to colleagues at the Royal Opera House, who patiently answered my questions; and to Rosemary Scoular, for her consistent support (over many years).

As ever, *The Oxford Dictionary of Dance* by Debra Craine and Judith Mackrell was an invaluable resource, as were G. B. L. Wilson's (older and now out-of-print) *Dictionary of Ballet* and Jennifer Homans's *Apollo's Angels*.

Finally, I would not have become a dancer without the influence of my mother, whose passion for ballet inspired my own. Heartfelt thanks to her; to my family, for staying in place while my career took me away; and to my friends and loved ones, for making sure I still find reasons to dance.